STUD

STUD

ADVENTURES
IN BREEDING

Kevin Conley

BLOOMSBURY

First published 2002 by Bloomsbury US,
175 Fifth Avenue, New York, N.Y. 10010
First published in Great Britain 2002 by Bloomsbury,
38 Soho Square, London, W1D 3HB

This paperback edition published 2003

A CIP catalogue record for this book is available from the British Library

ISBN 0 7475 6176 1

10 9 8 7 6 5 4 3 2 1

Typeset by Hewer Text Ltd, Edinburgh
Printed in Great Britain by Clays Ltd, St Ives plc

Contents

For my sire and dam

Introduction

THIS BOOK BEGINS at the happy ending, as the champion 'retires to stud'. Usually, those three words are the last you ever read about a favorite horse, buried in an agate-type item at the back of the sports section: 'Sir So and So has retired to stud.' To many men, the phrase presents an unattainable ideal, like 'assumed into heaven'.

At first glance, the stud's life sounds incredible, uniting three things rarely enjoyed all at once: retirement, plentiful sex, cash flow. When I began this story a couple of years ago, I was a newcomer to the horse world, armed with little more than shameless curiosity about what a stud really does. But the more I looked into the lifestyle, the more my amazement grew. There is no aspect of it that is less than it seems: the money is phenomenal, the sex is brisk and multifarious, and the settings are as green and unembarrassed as Eden.

Of course, there's already plenty of writing in the world about sex. There are studies and memoirs and picture books. But there's very little *reporting*, undertaken by disinterested parties, in wholesome surroundings, about sincere and uninhibited acts. It has been a great help that the participants in the acts recorded here were all horses, eager and consenting adults (for the most part) who did not seem the least bit bothered by having a reporter lurking in the shadows taking notes.

If you're like me, the sexual encounters of Thoroughbreds will look hugely different from anything in your personal experience. Nevertheless, after you've seen a few, you get used to the terrible, swift deed. You put aside fear (never all the way, but almost) and start to notice other things: intimate gestures and individual quirks. For the farm personnel who work in the breeding sheds, such attentiveness to character is part of the job. They have to know which stud is fast or shy or savage, who likes to dillydally on the grass and who needs a little extra squeeze at the decisive moment. They base their routines and schedules – even their survival – on the accuracy of these assessments of character.

The breeding of racehorses is a big business and a complicated one, driven by rich, impatient people and overseen by a cast of horse-country sophisticates equally adept at dealing with cool-headed sheikhs or mares in heat. But don't be distracted by equine legalese. The sexual act in all its mystery and brute mechanics lies at the heart of Thoroughbred breeding. There would be no story if I hadn't followed sires such as Storm Cat, Seattle Slew, Storm Boot, Cee's Tizzy, Danzig, and Devil Begone to their appointments in the breeding shed.

Following the sex life of horses can give a human some unlikely insights into his own odd habits. To the folks who work with horses, this can be a source of both laughter and wisdom. I would like to thank the people who were so generous with both: Doc Copelan and Randy Speakes; Wes Lanter of Overbrook Farm; Dan Rosenberg and Tom Wade at Three Chimneys; Karen and Mickey Taylor; Suzi Shoemaker of Lantern Hill Farm; the McLeans of Crestwood Farm; Gus Koch at Claiborne Farm; John Harris of Harris Ranch; Joan Rogers and Duane Griffith at Applebite Farms; Noreen Sullivan, of Jett Sport; Glenye Cain, at the *Daily Racing Form*; Nancy and Loren Bolinger of Running Horse Farm; and Sue McDonnell at the Havemeyer Equine Behavior Lab. They opened the gates and made the going easy.

ONE

A Stud's Life

MY FIRST CONTACT with the world's number-one stud at his place of business – that would be Storm Cat, at the stallion complex on W. T. Young's Overbrook Farm, in Lexington, Kentucky – came over the phone. 'There's his holler now,' Dr Joe Yocum, the farm vet, said calmly, from his office in the breeding shed, above a noise that sounded like the fury of hell. 'He just jumped on her. I'll look out my window here and tell you when he's finished . . . Yup.' The doctor chuckled. 'He wouldn't be real popular with the women.'

The Kentucky Derby is often called the most exciting two minutes in sports; Storm Cat is probably its most expensive thirty seconds. His stud fee for the 2002 season hit $500,000, nearly double that of his closest rival. A conservative estimate of fifty guaranteed-live-foal contracts suggests that Storm Cat will earn twenty million this year, after insurance. If he played in the NBA, that figure would make him the league's third-highest-paid player. As a stud, no one's even close.

Why would anyone pay that much for Storm Cat's services? In 1999, and 2000, Storm Cat's offspring earned more than $21 million dollars at the track, almost $7 million more than anyone else's. Furthermore, several Storm Cat colts who have recently launched their own stud careers – Storm Boot, Hennessy, Forest Wildcat – have begun siring stakes winners and high-priced yearlings, justifying hefty hikes in their stud fees. In other words, just thirty seconds with Storm Cat gives you a chance of landing your own franchise Thoroughbred. And many people who bring a mare to Storm Cat have more immediate plans for the offspring: at the 2001 yearling sales, Storm Cat babies sold for an average of $1.68 million.

If he were any other breed – miniature, trotter, quarter horse, Standardbred, Lipizzan, Arabian, American warmblood – Storm Cat could just jump on a padded phantom breeding mount (like a pommel horse, but 'natural, mare-like', and equipped with a 'side opening and quick release valve') and his half of the bargain could be frozen and shipped Priority Overnight to any mare in the world. But Storm Cat will never suffer this indignity, because the Jockey Club, the official registry of Thoroughbred racing, forbids artificial insemination. Only registered horses can race on the Thoroughbred circuit, and the Jockey Club registers only horses conceived by what is delicately termed 'natural cover'. Storm Cat's job – and the most profitable sector of a high-stakes industry – is safe.

Success at the track is merely a first step toward such profits. Take Cigar, who won sixteen races in a row and retired to stud in 1997, after earning a record $9.9 million. Not one of the eighty mares booked for his first and only season became pregnant, but his owners were lucky: Italy's Assicurazioni Generali made good on Cigar's $25 million infertility insurance policy. Far more common than infertility is mediocrity, and no policy covers the champion horse who fails to produce a winner. As Tom Wade, the groom to the 1977 Triple Crown winner, Seattle Slew, said, 'Just because a horse wins a million dollars, that don't make him no stud.'

For a stallion, the eagerness of a teenager is considered the mark of a professional – breeders call it 'great libido'. Although Storm Cat's libido is spoken of mostly in economic terms, from time to time something else creeps in: awe, fear, relief. Breeding horses is dangerous – in March, 2000, Class Secret, a twelve-year-old son of Secretariat, the 1973 Triple Crown winner, had to be euthanized after a mare he was mounting broke his leg – so dawdling is not appreciated. It's risky for the people involved, too. One stallion manager told me that sildenafil citrate – Viagra – had been tested on horses and rejected, largely because nobody who works in the breeding shed wants to fool around with a rearing, half-ton, hormonally enraged animal trying to set a personal endurance record.

With a horse like Storm Cat, however, the worrying doesn't stop at the breeding shed. He's only eighteen years old, comfortably mid-career for a stud (Mr Prospector, the sire of the 2000 Derby winner, Fusaichi Pegasus, was twenty-nine when he died in 1999). But even innocent conversations about him – what he likes to eat (bluegrass, oats, and sweet feed), where he sleeps (in a hilltop barn, near his winter paddock), what he does for fun (lies down in a big sandpile and rolls around) – tend to veer into elaborately imagined premonitions of his death and the state-of-the-art precautions taken to guard against it. One of his sandpiles, for example, is bounded by an unusual stretch of solid wood, because somebody worried that he might roll a foreleg under the standard fencing and break a bone as he tried to stand up. And if you want to meet the farm's entire staff in the next forty seconds? Just light a cigarette near Storm Cat's stall.

On a sunny morning in May, halfway through the four-and-a-half-month breeding season, the sire looks vigorous. In his official photographs, Storm Cat can come across as smug and bullnecked and a little thick in the waist, but the camera must add a few pounds, because in person, prancing in his paddock, he has the hauteur and the low body fat of an underwear model. He's a dark bay, but when he moves in the sunlight you can pick up flashes of a honey-gold color that comes from the chestnut horses on his mother's side – Terlingua, Storm Cat's dam (his mother), and his grandsire,

Secretariat. He has white spats on his left legs, also from Terlingua, which give him a light-footed, high-stepping look, even when he's just pacing over the grass.

'I like his weight now,' Wes Lanter, who manages the ten stallions at Overbrook Farm, says. 'Twelve hundred and sixty pounds. I think that's a real good weight for him.' Lanter runs the operations in the breeding shed with the nimbleness of a linebacker coach, but everywhere else he moves with hound-dog-like deliberateness. To introduce me to the planet's most valuable piece of horseflesh, for example, he folds his arms and says, 'There he is.' At first, Storm Cat just rips at the grass, pretending he doesn't see us, but after a while he edges over to the fence to investigate. He has a smoldering dark patch between his eyes with a white diamond on it, and a sharp crescent moon way over near his left nostril, a curious marking that makes him look moody and dangerously attractive. He ducks his head behind a board on the fence and gives me the once-over – more eye contact than his mares usually get – and I raise my hand to the little white line that runs down his muzzle. 'Stand back,' Lanter says, since stallions bite. 'He can fool you.' As soon as I touch him, Storm Cat ends the interview and walks away.

Suddenly, he lights out for the end of his paddock. Through a break in the trees, he looks over the creek, past the horses nearer the breeding shed – it's standard practice to place stallions with libidos lower than Storm Cat's closer to the parade of action, a cheap stimulant that cuts down on the time spent waiting for arousal – and roars convincingly. 'A mare has arrived,' Lanter says. 'Not yours, Stormy.' Undeterred, Storm Cat paces back and forth beside the fence – he has worn a path there – and roars again. Lanter seems pleased, in a proud and wistful prom-chaperon way. 'He's looking for dates,' he says.

Storm Cat has seven hundred and fourteen children at last count, but he has seen only four: Tabasco Cat (the winner of the Preakness and the Belmont in 1994) and Mountain Cat, who were recently shipped off to Japan and Turkey, respectively, and two fellow studs on the roster at Overbrook Farm – Tactical Cat, a pretty gray horse (whose dam was Terre Haute), and the freshman stallion Cat Thief (whose dam was Train Robbery). They often pass each other on the way to or from the breeding shed, and he cuts them every time – no nicker, no friendly whinny. Apart from a few pointed, work-related roars, Storm Cat is laconic, even for a horse. But his is a menacing, eloquent silence: it's on purpose.

Menace, apparently, is a job requirement for stallions. The senior managers at Overbrook, who generally live in picturesque houses tucked into the farm's manicured hills, like to expound upon the equine instinct for violence. They'll tell you how, in the wild, a lone stallion would command a roving harem cum nursery of broodmares and foals, until some other horse, probably one of his own sons, decided to bite, kick, and break his legs for it. Add to these instincts a few centuries of breeding specifically for aggressiveness – a trait Storm Cat is prized for and seems to be able to pass on to his foals – and you have the potential for some very volatile relationships.

That's the theory. In practice, Storm Cat – apart from his twice-daily acts of sexual congress with the fastest, wealthiest, and most attractive available partners in the world, seven days a week throughout the breeding season – lives like a monk. He eats mostly grass, sleeps on straw, drinks only water. He has no visits with the other stallions. His one diversion is running away from his groom, which he is doing less of lately, because his current groom is kind but strict. He wears only a leather halter. He does not race, he does not train for racing, he does not even exercise. He has given all that up.

Regularly, en route to the breeding shed, he steps on a scale. If the number seems high, he cuts back on the sweet feed that is his sole indulgence. His weight is monitored minutely. When he dropped a few pounds in February, at the beginning of the breeding season, he was rushed to the Hagyard Davidson and McGee Veterinary Clinic, in Lexington. 'It wasn't much – enterocolitis,' Doc Yocum said. 'With any other horse, we probably wouldn't have bothered.' He traced its onset to a few instances when Storm Cat arrived at the breeding shed wringing wet before he even started: 'My theory is he was just so worked up to get back at the mares.'

Storm Cat's stall – where he goes as infrequently as possible, to get his coat brushed, say, or to sleep during inclement weather – is outwardly unremarkable: a foot and a half of straw in a whitewashed cinder-block room with two wooden doors. (Even here, value creates value: Storm Cat's muck is carted off and resold to the Campbell's Soup Company, which uses it as the breeding ground for the mushrooms in its mushroom soup.) But while he sleeps, a box nestled in the ridge of his barn projects an infrared beam that looks for obscurity – smoke. An ultraviolet device picks up flickers of light in the hydrocarbon range – flame. A third mechanism compares ambient temperature against its rate of rise – heat. These three devices monitoring the separate elements of fire are tied into the forty-second alarm system and into a sprinkler system, fed by massive pipes capable of delivering six inches of standing water to the stall in seconds. Fire is a problem because barns are drafty by design and straw is extremely flammable, but Ben Giles, who guides the building projects at the farm, compares Overbrook's safeguards favorably with fire detection measures in museums. 'We don't have the luxury of being able to cut a barn up into small spaces to confine or suppress a fire, because a horse needs air. In that sense, the museums have it a little easier,' Giles says. 'Plus, their van Goghs are worth a whole lot less than Storm Cat.'

It took a long time for people to see that Storm Cat was a lucky horse. As a yearling, he was smallish, longhaired, potbellied, with turned-out knees that got him booted out of Kentucky's best auction. Twice at the track, he lost races that he should have won, once because he shouldered an inferior horse in the final stretch out of sheer cussedness, and later because his mind wandered when he was too far in front at the Breeders' Cup, a race that would have established him as the leading contender for two-year-old horse of the year. He missed all his Triple Crown races as a three-year-old because he was recovering from knee surgery, and when he tried to come back, late in the year, he trained on dirt that had turned greasy after a hard rain, and was never the same. When he retired from racing, in 1988, people quickly forgot about him. His stud fee dropped from $30,000 to $25,000 to $20,000, and he couldn't fill his book of mares.

Then his first crop of colts and fillies hit the track. Suddenly, people started remembering what a brilliant, blazingly fast runner he'd been, how he took a competitive streak that bordered on the criminal and used it to overcome his natural unsoundness. By the time his second and third crops hit, people knew that Storm Cats could run. They could run at two years old, or three, or four; colts or fillies, they could run long or short, turf or dirt, in Europe, Japan, or America. By 1994, when Tabasco Cat took the last two jewels of the Triple Crown, it was clear that Storm Cat had a calling.

The mares arrive for their appointments by horse van and walk over a gravel loading dock into the receiving barn – a sort of greenroom for mares in estrus. When a mare enters, somebody pushes a button, a window opens, and Cooperstown, an Overbrook teaser stallion, sticks his head in to try his luck, nuzzling her flank and nosing her haunches. If she kicks, he's the one she kicks at, not Storm Cat. ('If they don't make it at the track, they end up being teasers,' Doc Yocum says. 'So it's a little incentive deal.') In the past twenty years, veterinarians have grown very precise in pinpointing ovulation (an increase in accuracy that has allowed stallions to double their workload – and farms to double their profits – since fewer and fewer mares require follow-up visits), but final verification is still left to the teaser stallion. If there are any doubts about her receptivity after Cooperstown's initial interview, he is forced to try a jump himself – wearing a leather butcher's apron to insure that the dry run goes unconsummated. Usually, though, she's willing, the window shuts for Coop, and the mare is led into a padded chute to be washed for the breeding shed.

Just before Storm Cat's mare is ready, his groom, Filemon Martinez, a quiet man with a Clark Gable mustache, walks the sire of sires across a covered bridge over Hickman Creek to the stallion barn. From the doorway of the barn, where Storm Cat and Martinez wait like actors in the wings, you can hear the business of breeding: 'Easy, boss,' and 'Go, buddy,' and, if it's a stallion with problems in the Valentino department, the pacesetting shouts of 'Hyup! Hyup! Hyup!' Most do just fine in the breeding shed, although farm policy seems to be 'Anywhere that works'. At least one stallion, Cape Town, prefers to perform al fresco, on the grass, with all the usual team in attendance, plus one guy giving helpful pushes from the rear.

By the time Storm Cat enters the shed, the video camera is rolling (for lawsuits and insurance) and the mare – Rootentootenwooten, in this case – is standing with her head against the wall, wearing padded booties on both hind feet. Storm Cat neighs or hollers or roars – whatever it is, it's frightening and long and full of the inevitable, like the squeal of tires that you know will end in shattering glass. Then he measures himself and rears while the team rushes around him. There are two schools of natural cover: pasture breeding, where horses are let loose in a paddock together, and hand breeding, where a squad of breeding-shed professionals choreo-graph the proceedings for safety and speed. Overbrook prefers the latter, as practically all large-scale breeding operations do, and their version of it takes at least five people: two to soothe and distract the mare, one to steady the stallion, a tail man, and the stallion manager. When Storm Cat rears, the tail man lifts up the mare's tail, and Wes Lanter, wearing a latex glove, pilots Storm Cat to the place he probably would have found on his own, but not as quickly.

All the majesty of the act is in the roaring, apparently – count to fifteen and it's over. Somebody says 'Good cover' with a mixture of appreciation and relief, and Storm Cat, still draped across Rootentootenwooten's back, fits the curl of his neck to hers and allows himself a moment of unstallionlike tenderness before he backs off and puts his feet on the ground again. The stallion manager pulls down a handheld shower nozzle, of the sort you find in French bathtubs, to wash Storm Cat off. Then the groom leads the sire away, through the stallion barn, down the hill, and back into the shadows of the covered bridge. Lanter pulls off his latex glove and says, 'He's what everybody hopes happens to them when they retire.'

TWO

Bidding Wars

STORM CAT MAKES his millions in the breeding shed, but he gets his headlines at the sales. 'Hip number 356,' the auctioneer says, as some nervous yearling with a sticker (on his hip) follows a ringman in a coat, tie, and leather gloves – at the Keeneland sales in Lexington, Kentucky, the job invariably goes to a small and dignified black guy – out of the walking ring and into the sales pavilion. From a wooden barricade eight feet above the horse, the auctioneer announces the provenance in a stately radio basso, a little family history before he takes a minute to turn horseflesh into cash.

If he says, 'A chestnut colt, by Storm Cat, out of Hum Along,' or 'A mare, in foal to the leading sire Storm Cat', the bidspotters, who travel the auction circuit from Lexington and Saratoga to England and Puerto Rico, do a quick check on the house. It's no secret where the sheikhs sit: nearly everyone in the entourage of Sheikh Mohammed Bin Rashid Al Maktoum, the crown prince of Dubai and the defense minister general of the United Arab Emirates, wears royal-blue windbreakers. Across the auditorium, the big-money Irish buyers – you can say 'the boys', and horse traders will know who you mean – peer out at the horse between their reading glasses and their battered Panama hats.

Most of the buyers in the pavilion – Kentucky breeders, English bookies, Irish vets, Florida pinhookers, Hall-of-Fame trainers, bloodstock agents for owners in Hong Kong – could give you a fair estimate of what nearly every horse should sell for. They've been prepping for weeks, visiting farms and going through their routine: assessing conformation, checking the articulation of the knee joints and the angle of the hooves, looking over the thirty-two X rays stored in the sales repository, or just going back to the barns on the sales grounds to watch the hips of the yearlings as they walk down the shedrows ('See that swing,' a Bourbon County vet told me. 'That's the way you want a horse to look. Like a high-school girl').

But if the boys and the sheikhs have their eye on the same horse, you can throw out the estimates. The four Maktoums – the Doobie Brothers, as they're called in Lexington – descend from a branch of Bani Yas camel raiders who extorted protection money from nineteenth-century merchant caravans. Today, they rule Dubai, the second-wealthiest of the seven Arab Emirates; the oldest brother is worth more than $10 billion. The crown prince, the family's most accomplished horseman, who regularly rides endurance horses in hundred-mile races through the desert, is the chief bidder for a family that has spent more than $600 million at the Keeneland sales alone.

The boys – the fifty-two-year-old Irish breeder John Magnier (who descends from a branch of County Cork dairy and stud farmers), and his backups, the retired bookie Michael Tabor and the vet Demi O'Byrne – like to think of themselves as continuing a great Irish tradition, what Magnier calls 'the instinctive under-standing the Irish have of the horses'. Coolmore Stud, head-quartered in Fethard, in County Tipperary, in the shadow of Sliabh na mBan (that's Gaelic for 'Mountain of the Women'), runs the world's largest stallion and racing outfit, with stud farms and training centers in Ireland, Australia, and Kentucky. Their dominance in the breeding industry is partly subsidized by Irish tax incentives – stud fees, the most profitable segment of any Thoroughbred enterprise, are tax exempt under a law introduced in 1968 by Charles Haughey, who later became prime minister. This advantage allows Coolmore to consolidate its hold on the best Thoroughbred bloodlines by acquiring racing prospects in both up and down markets, in a sort of equine version of dollar-cost averaging.

One Irish talent that eludes the boys is the gift of the gab: after Haughey appointed him to the Irish Senate in 1987, Magnier spoke on the record only three times in three years. The Coolmore crowd maintains an almost comical silence with the press (Q: Did you ever consider dropping out of the bidding war? A: Yeah). This is partly strategy – bidding at auctions is, like poker, a game of calculated bluffing based largely on an unwavering policy of disinformation – and partly paranoia verging on megalomania. Even Magnier's art buyer, Matthew Green, operated under a vow of silence when he acquired *The Proud Galloper*, a painting by Jack Butler Yeats, for the Magniers, who own houses in Switzerland, Spain, and Barbados, and companies in Ireland, the Dutch Antilles, the Cayman Islands, and other tax-sheltering isles.

Do the regular pissing matches between the Doobie Brothers and the Coolmore boys appeal to the Kentucky crowd? When Magnier and Sheikh Mohammed and their entourages file into their assigned seats at Keeneland, all the noise and excess testosterone drain out of the halls around the sales pavilion, and the crowds return to the auction ring. The men employed by auction houses to spot bids promptly – a group of old hands known as bidspotters – prowl the aisles. They know the quirks of the regulars (the guy who bids with a casual wave, the one who'll keep going till he uncrosses his legs). These bidspotters peer over their assigned sections of the pavilion, looking for the sign that says, 'I'm in.'

As soon as a bidspotter spots one, he yells 'Hyah!' with the professional theatrics of a home-plate ump. Across the hall, another spotter answers. A tote board keeps track of the chant of the auctioneer, who keeps pace with the bidspotters, who keep scanning the crowd, and when the bidding sails past the million-dollar mark with no sign of slowing, the photographers in the press box look up from their golf books and computer solitaire to readjust their focus.

The people buying the best horses – your kings and sheikhs and tax exiles – don't have to check their stock portfolios every morning to see what they can afford. This is not breaking news. But it's still real money, and if you're down at Keeneland, it's hard not to translate the gargantuan bidding into personal terms. To me, an apartment-dwelling New Yorker, it sounded like: 'I got a ONE-bedroom, who'll give me floor-through? Two-bedroom walkup, sir, do I hear DUPLEX? Cobble Hill duplex – BROWNSTONE, Brooklyn. Who's got WEST SIDE! Riverview, threebaths, doorman! PARK Ave, Seventies, summer at the SEAshore. SPIELBERG next door, private gym and heliport.' And so on – more than a hundred and fifty million dollars' worth of horses in the first two days of the September sale.

By the time hip number 356 – that chestnut colt by Storm Cat out of the Fappiano mare Hum Along – walked into the ring on the second day of the September sales, I thought I had acclimated to the high-altitude numbers. The day before, Sheikh Mohammed had bought a Pulpit colt for $2.3 million; the Canadian track owner Frank Stronach paid $2.2 million for a colt by A. P. Indy; and another A. P. Indy set a record for yearling fillies at the September sale, at $2.15 million. Bloodstock agents were saying that even these numbers seemed low, and a lot of buyers expecting higher prices hadn't bothered to vet the best horses. Now they were making frantic calls to their clients and scrambling to check out the suddenly affordable-ish stock. Another faction was saying, *Wait. Just wait.*

By day two of the sales, I could easily fall asleep to the drone of the bidding. This is partly because the auctioneers use a singsong cadence with a lot of hoppita-boppita verbal spackling to fill in the seconds between bids. Thrilling if it's your money, I'm sure, but otherwise it can sound like central air. The other reason I kept snoozing let's call the Intro to Physics principle: the bidding was really tough to follow. First of all, you had to know who did what for whom. For instance, even though the Coolmore money comes from Magnier and Tabor (and who knows how many even more silent partners), Demi O'Byrne acts as their bloodstock agent and does much of the actual bidding (although other Coolmore agents have been known to bid from elsewhere in the pavilion). But O'Byrne is not required to perform an athletic act to lodge a bid: if he were so inclined, he could set up a signal that only a bidspotter would notice, like adjusting his reading glasses. Once you learn that, any signature fidget can look like a legitimate bid. And the bidding is fast. And not all the bidders are in the room – the Europeans, especially, like to bid from out back, where the horses are led in and out of the auction ring and you can smoke. And the bids may not even be real – you can't tell when an auctioneer is manufacturing bids to speed the process past a seller's reserve price. Even the bidders themselves aren't always sure of the action. Afterward they'll tell you, 'I think I was in at three hundred thousand. But don't quote me. I don't know.'

Each auctioneer has his own style, but most open the bidding by tossing out an astronomical figure, say, $500,000, which he quickly lowers ('Who'll give meTWOnow, ONEhundredthousand?'), until he gets in range of numbers that make sense on earth. But a few times a session, somebody hooks on to that opening space shot right away – which is what happened with hip number 356. 'Hyah!' Five, six, seven hundred thousand – bidders seemed to be jumping in all over the floor. Around one million or a million-one, the pace steadied a bit. Maybe it was the bargain hunters dropping out. Maybe the bloodstock agents were waiting for service on their cellular phones.

As the tote board headed toward two million, the people milling about the Keeneland corridors, which have all the clique awareness and random body contact of a high-school class change, started crowding the picture windows around the sales pavilion. At this point, David Shimmon, the x-factor California tech exec – at Saratoga the month before, he'd come out of nowhere to bid $4.2 million for a Seattle Slew colt – sensed a lull in the bidding. He interpreted it as hesitation, and he jumped in, thinking that bidders were losing heart. He thought he could scare off the stragglers with an aggressive entry and a burst of rapid-fire bids. He stuck it out for a while, for a few bids in the $2 million range. Then the man who'd spent more for an unraced horse than anybody else that year dropped out, too.

This left three bidders: Demi O'Byrne, sitting with the Coolmore clan at the back left of the amphitheater; Sheikh Mohammed, fourth row center, with a chatty entourage of about ten; and D. Wayne Lukas, the silver-haired Hall-of-Fame trainer, alone on an aisle seat to the right, bidding for Satish Sanan, who was present by virtue of a cell phone that Lukas only rarely consulted. Each of the men is considered a keen judge of promise in a one-year-old horse, and each of them must have gained confidence from the presence of the others. The industry depends on just this sort of mutual admiration: you can't fight a bidding war alone.

It wasn't just the buyers practicing gamesmanship – it had taken quite a bit just to get this horse to the auction ring. Hip number 356 was born close to the end of foaling season, on June 2, 1999. His promise seemed obvious almost immediately – the colt came into the world with a Storm Cat engine on long, straight Hum Along legs. But his late birth put him at a disadvantage. He was sure to be too small for Keeneland's select yearling sale the next July – he'd look scrawny compared to the January colts – so Will Farish, the breeder who owns and runs Lane's End, where the colt was born, decided to hold on to him till the September sale.

Lane's End is a Kentucky showcase – Queen Elizabeth stays there when she comes to Kentucky to look at stallions – but it's more like a college than a farm. They stand twenty-two stallions; they board more than two hundred mares; they sell anywhere from forty to sixty head at nearly every Keeneland sale. Farish doesn't own all these horses, of course, but he directs the farm's policy, consults with the owners, acts as agent for the farm's roster of syndicated stallions. Like a football coach from an earlier era – picture somebody natty and decisive, like Bear Bryant – he's the public face of the powerhouse. (Farish, a former polo player with Texas roots – that is, Standard Oil – is also a longtime Republican fund-raiser and friend of Bush *père et fils*: when the elder Bush put his fortune into a blind trust during his presidency, Farish managed the trust. His loyalty and generosity were rewarded when the junior Bush appointed him ambassador to the United Kingdom, in July 2001.)

Farish noticed the horse early. By the time the foal was six weeks old, he paid an undisclosed sum to the owner, Ted Taylor, for a half-interest. A year later, in an apparently unconnected move, he held the entire consignment of Lane's End yearlings – including his Storm Cat-Hum Along colt – out of the July sale. Historically, the July sale attracts the best racing prospects, who bring the year's highest prices, while the September sales lag behind. But by holding back his whole crop (following a trend set by other Keeneland consigners), Farish could almost force the buyers to come to him. He was betting that his September consignment – ninety-five colts and eighty-five fillies, at final count – would bring out the buyers no matter when he chose to sell them.

Thanks to such maneuvers, hip number 356 was in good company and strategically positioned to bring the best possible price. On the Friday before the sales, he arrived at Barn 20, up on the hill above the sales pavilion, four days before he was scheduled to step into the auction ring. Like all the Lane's End horses, he was well prepared. He was familiar with the prodding and parading that was required of him – potential buyers had been visiting for months, picking up his hooves, making him walk down and back, down and back, down and back. And after two full summers out on the Kentucky bluegrass, the Storm Cat colt had caught up to his peers. He was big and built and looked the part. His conformation was close to perfect. It didn't hurt that he was also pretty – on the golden side of chestnut, with the big friendly blaze you see painted on carousel ponies, and a hunk of bangs he kept boyishly tossing out of his eyes, like a Baja beach hunk.

But no sales team could prepare him for the scene he saw now, as he stood on a stage scarcely bigger than a stall. Only two ropes separated the colt from a seven-hundred-seat theater. Had the place been empty, the layout might have soothed him: the ceiling was peaked high as a barn's; the walls and the vast wood-beam arches were the color of straw; and the seats – even the exit signs – were pasture green. But Keeneland was anything but empty now and the eight double doors kept opening, bringing more and more rubberneckers down the aisles toward him. As he turned to investigate, the colt stepped in and out of the bright lights (even at this final hour, the buyers are evaluating the stock; hip number 356's imperious air in front of the Keeneland buyers was a good sign of how he'd react to the roaring crowds at the track). His coat had been brushed and oiled with Show Sheen before he left his stall, so the overhead spots picked out the glint of his muscle bundles braiding and unbraiding nervously as the ringman tugged his shank to steady him.

Now, as the bidding passed three million dollars, D. Wayne Lukas dropped out, leaving only the two stalwarts who faced each other at almost every sale. The pace of the bidding changed. Neither party was going to be scared off by a few rapid-fire bids. In steady hundred-thousand dollar increments, they seesawed past a figure the Coolmore team knew well – the four-million mark, the point where two years earlier Magnier had abandoned a bidding war with the Japanese venture capitalist Fusao Sekiguchi over a Mr Prospector yearling. That colt, Fusaichi Pegasus, ended up winning six races in nine starts, including the 2000 Kentucky Derby, and in June, Coolmore took part in a second, private bidding war for him, in hopes of acquiring his services as a stud. This time they won, but it cost them somewhere in the vicinity of $60 million. Magnier, already systematically ruthless when it came to acquiring horses, emerged from the 'Fu Peg' experience with an expensive reminder of the high cost of hesitation.

'Six million, now we're gettin' serious,' the auctioneer said. He and the colt seemed to grow more comfortable as the tension mounted in the hall, and at $6.4 million, the horse turned his hindquarters to the audience, lifted his tail, and offered two hefty volleys in evidence of his digestive soundness, a gesture of almost regal indifference aimed, coincidentally, directly at the Sheikh. Perhaps that was when Sheikh Mohammed realized that this was a battle he might be better off losing. He made two more bids, then let Coolmore take the horse. At $6.8 million, the final bid was more than anyone had paid for a horse at auction since 1985, at the height of the Bluegrass Bubble, when Seattle Dancer sold for $13.1 million. (The Bluegrass Bubble is the name given to the mid-eighties speculative boom in Thoroughbred bloodstock, which had the same crazy rise and sudden crash as tulips in seventeenth-century Holland or dot-coms in the nineties.) As the gavel fell, the auctioneer quickly warned the audience, 'Please hold your applause till the horse is out of the ring.' Then he added, 'We'd like to thank Demi O'Byrne and Sheikh Mohammed for their vigorous bidding.' As the ringman led the colt out, a man in straw-colored coveralls emerged with a broom.

The Sheikh and his entourage left the sales pavilion en masse, a hasty exodus of blue jeans and windbreakers that seemed peevish in the circumstances, although the team recovered quickly, spending $5.3 million that afternoon on hip number 560, another Lane's End colt — 'a lovely individual', according to the Sheikh, and one he considered better than the sales-topper, which is what they all say when they lose.

The trade reporters hustled over for the fruitless postacquisition interview with Demi O'Byrne, who submitted to the charade with a pained and medicinal expression that is apparently not his natural one. Reports from patrons of McCarthy's — the Lexington pub owned by O'Byrne's brother and named after a Fethard hotel where the lads celebrate a victory over rounds of Black Velvets, a mixture of Guinness and champagne — suggest that the handsome forty-nine-year-old vet can be a devilish comrade, with a taste for roistering.

Despite the dour faces on the victorious party, the pavilion filled with a general festiveness. As Farish fielded congratulations, somebody good-naturedly asked, 'Do you pay Demi now or later?' People with no connection whatsoever to the sale were celebrating, rehashing the event, speculating about its implications, or hurrying out to Cell Phone Hill beside the sales pavilion to call their friends. Even though I knew no one remotely interested in the auction watershed, I, too, retreated there and began to impose the news on my wife and friends — who answered my calls with an indifference that helped speed my reintegration into the real world. On the way back to the pavilion, I stopped at a refreshment stand run by Turf Catering and ordered an iced lemonade. 'That'll be four hundred and fifty thousand,' the salesgirl said. I gave her a five.

THREE

From Kazakhstan to the
Breeders' Cup

LONG BEFORE HORSES were risky multimillion-dollar investments, they were meat. The horse is well adapted to cold climates – wild horses can graze contented and unconcerned with snow piling up on their backs. And for millennia, the people who lived in such cold climates, from Eastern Europe to Mongolia, hunted and ate horses. In some areas of Kazakhstan, horsemeat is still highly prized, the sort of special-occasion treat you'd serve at a wedding. And there is a long local tradition of clever use of the horse and horse by-products: the ancestors of the Kazakhs not only ate the meat, they drank the fermented milk. They made a gelatinous soup of the hooves. They collected the sweat as a medicinal supplement, a sort of proto-Gatorade. They used the tendons and sinews for strong thread. They discovered a substance in the brain that could be rubbed into horse leather to make it supple.

Every summer now, archaeologists come to Kazakhstan to un-earth the chronology of domestication. They dig for horse bones, trying to establish slaughtering patterns, and they always seem to come to the conclusion that the vast majority of the bones belong to adult horses. This is taken as evidence that the strongest specimens were carefully set aside to ride. But such population studies are still circumstantial evidence. Hard evidence, like bridles, cinches, or saddle blankets, seems to have disappeared, decayed with the rest of the flesh.

With so little to go on, the conjectures of archaeologists take on the qualities of fiction; they can feel truer than history. History, with its wealth of coins and vases and regal seals, tells us, emphatically and somewhat absurdly, that the complicated business of driving a chariot preceded the simpler option of just getting on the back of the horse and riding. This developmental sequence ('*fahren und reiten*', according to German scholars) is apparently well established by artwork and the documentary evidence of classical civilizations: by 1500 BC, warriors driving chariots show up in India, in Iran, in northern Syria, in China. But some archaeologists sketch a different story, one that begins as much as a thousand years earlier, at the outskirts of human settlement, where the poorer tribal populations of the Eurasian steppes came in contact with another subsistence species. Both of them were trying to get by in scrubland.

Those people, like the poor everywhere, had little to leave behind; they were shepherds and subsistence farmers. And when their food supply dwindled, especially in the winter, they killed and ate horses. But this meant that they also studied them, following them to survive. They knew that horses could break through ice with their hooves to get water. And they knew that horses could push their noses through the snow to find pasture. They knew that horses would do both of these things at times when their own idiot sheep would just stand in two inches of snow and starve.

It is hard to establish when people stopped hunting horses and instead began to keep them like cattle, a step that apparently preceded riding. But certainly the biggest change came at the point when some brave soul jumped on the back of a horse. After that, the hardiest specimens were spared, for hunting and rustling and raiding.

Once these poor shepherds could ride, they discovered that the largely uninhabitable scrubland of the steppes could act as the fuel for an economic revolution, which apparently worked like this: One man alone can look after about two hundred sheep. One man on horseback can look after five hundred. And a tribe of horsemen can turn a half a continent of empty grassland too poor and windswept for agriculture into a source of wealth just as vast as anything you could produce by farming a fertile valley.

In this scenario, the horse and rider conquer the world not by warcraft but by wealth. Linguists have a line of historical conjecture that matches the archaeologists': they've imagined a language that began to spread out of roughly the same area of Eurasia where archaeologists believe riding began. Traces of that language, which linguists call proto-Indo-European, appear in English, Hindi, Russian, Baltic, German, Greek, Italian, French, Swedish; the horses coming out of the steppes carried not only the riders but their language as well.

By the time that horse and driver show up in history, the wealth they've amassed requires armies, and the armies have chariots, and the chariots are everywhere: in Iran, in northern Syria, in Greece, in India. History had begun, built on the way a horse can cover ground.

3,500 years later, horses are everywhere in the Lexington landscape. There are, of course, the horse farms, horse hospitals, and horse parks with their miles and miles of wooden fences, converted tobacco barns, and old Kentucky homes. That's just to start. There are horses in horse vans on the highways and back roads, horse statues on the roadside and at the post office, framed photos of horse tack in the hotel rooms, horseshoes on the bathroom doors in bars, the names of champion horses – Citation, Sir Barton, Alysheba – on the streets. There's an auto repair shop called the Car Jockey, a software company called Horse Cents, a restaurant called Furlongs that specializes in Cajun food and sports a flashing Budweiser sign in the window showing a horse and jockey at full gallop. There's an Equus Run Vineyards and a discount liquor store called the Thoroughbred Shop. The biggest Ford dealership is Man O' War Ford. There's an assisted-living home called the Preakness. And so on, unto death.

Kentucky calls itself the Bluegrass State; but really of the state's hundred and twenty counties, only six – Bourbon, Fayette, Jessamine, Madison, Scott, and Woodford – count as prime horse country. This small and geologically favored region, the inner bluegrass, sits on a plain of limestone and shale, the oldest bedrock in the state. The rock in this mineral-rich layer consists, essentially, of bazillions of seashells, laid down during a warm snap of seventy million years when Kentucky's climate was much like Bermuda's today. All those seashells, buried for the four hundred million more years it took to crush them into limestone, now lie close to the surface of the earth again.

Horses thrive on this land for a few reasons. First, the limestone is rich in calcium, which finds its way into the bluegrass, and then into the bones of Thoroughbreds. Horses grazing on such power pasture grow more quickly because of it, and when they get to the track, the theory goes, their calcium-rich bones tend to break down less. So they run more fearlessly and win more often than horses bred in places where the main vegetation is saguaro, say, or cranberry bogs.

There's another benefit from all that buried limestone. As the ground water circulates through it, the minerals dissolve. Over the millennia, subterranean streams carve out caves in the bedrock. As these caves collapse under the weight of the earth, the land above them takes on the gently rolling appearance you see in horse country. Gentle hills are ideal for expensive horses. But drive about thirty miles from downtown Lexington in any direction, and the limestone is cut through with other rocks, in combinations that create a different terrain: just outside the inner bluegrass, the hills are steeper, the pasture is poorer, and the footing is far too dangerous for the tender, twistable ankles of the Thoroughbred.

There are other compelling reasons why Lexington is the world's horse capital (as one Yankee bloodstock agent put it, 'That's where the semen is'), but the wealth of limestone is the most ancient one, and as you head west from Lexington on Route 64, you see plenty of it exposed in the roadside escarpments that the Army Corps of Engineers had to blast through to make the highway. Just past Frankfort, you come to a fallen-rock zone where manmade bluffs of limestone tower above the two westbound lanes like a canyon. Here, you pass out of the inner bluegrass, and the land changes from almost pure horse farm to a more Yoknapatowphan mix of agriculture. You see cows and sheep, barbed wire and fallen fences, an occasional rusted boat parked by a tree, rivers and forests and ravines giving way to scattered industry, interstate eateries, and train yards. And then you drive down into the Ohio River valley into Louisville, to a place where, as they say in Kentucky, the horses run a hole in the wind.

From the roof of Churchill Downs, on the morning of the 2000 Breeders' Cup Championship, you could look out at the whole bowl of the valley, smokestacks lining the bend of the river, bridges going over it. It was the first Saturday in November, so the trees still had their fall colors, muted by the gray day. There were hills in the distance, and above the horizon, here and there, you could look through the crisscrossing ironwork of the roller coaster at Six Flags Kentucky Kingdom. All day long, planes on their descent into Louisville International Airport flew right over Papa Johns Cardinals Stadium, across the street from the track. The horses didn't seem to notice.

Before the races began, a flag team from a local high school practiced among the picnickers on the infield. Around noon, Paul Patton, the governor of Kentucky, stepped out of a gazebo to offer a welcome, which was met with indifference. The crowd saved its fervor for the jockeys, the twenty or so best in the country, who lined up in single file down the stretch, facing the grandstand in their colorful silks – hot pink, orange with a blue 'B', black with a gold sash, blue with a yellow diamond, white with a green chevron, purple with a pink-diamond frame. When they were introduced, the younger jocks stepped forward with a confident wave, and the older guys mostly just nodded and accepted the adulation.

The Breeders' Cup Championship began in 1984, during the flush times of the Bluegrass Bubble, when the owners and breeders were raking in millions, selling yearlings and stallion syndications and setting new world records at it practically every month. John Gaines, of Gainesway Farm, one of the fanciest spreads in Kentucky at the time, convinced his fellow breeders to create the world's richest day of racing, a slate of seven races with purses that started at a million dollars. The breeders funded it with a sort of self-imposed tax: every year, farms donated the cost of one service for every stallion on their roster. They also paid a qualifying fee for every foal, in an amount that was minimal at birth (about five hundred dollars), but grew increasingly hefty as the horse started winning.

Today, the Breeders' Cup functions as a sort of unofficial opening of the breeding season. Although the purses are huge, for the breeders they're almost beside the point. Most racing stables run their operations at or near a loss. While a win can go a long way to putting them snugly in the black, the real payoff for a Breeders' Cup win comes in the breeding shed. Both the winner and his sire easily fill their book with quality mares, and many farms wait for the day's results before finalizing stud fees, especially for their first-year stallions fresh off the track. Overbrook, for example, announced before the race that Cat Thief, the winner of the 1999 Classic, would stand at $60,000 if he won it again, and $35,000 if he didn't.

The breeders had fortunes riding on these races. The racing press, on the other hand, made actual bets; the row of wagering windows in the press box were not intended as a courtesy gesture, like the buffalo wings in the press canteen. The twelve hundred credentialed writers, photographers, radio correspondents, sound engineers, cameramen, and union electricians covering the Breeders' Cup did a brisk business at the windows, and as you walked through the warren of desks and teleports, you'd hear them trading tips and testing out their research with their peers.

'I've got Kona Gold and Trippi.'

'Ladies Din I feel pretty good about for prices.'

'Oxley's horse. I won the exacta. Close to a thousand dollars – Hold on. I've got to thank the guy that pointed out a horse to me.'

Before the first Breeders' Cup race, for fillies and mares three years old and up, a pair of Kentucky writers traded imaginary race calls. In the younger man's call, Riboletta, who'd won her last six races and was widely regarded as the only sure thing of the day, ran well down the stretch only to be nosed out by a filly listed at 56–1. 'At the wire, it's SPAIN!' he said, and the two men laughed at the unlikelihood – a brief, grumpy chortle in grudging appreciation of the overwhelming favorite. But when the horses ran, Riboletta faded to seventh and Spain actually did win, bringing the second-highest payoff in the sixteen-year history of the Breeders' Cup – a return of $113.80 on a two-dollar bet. The younger man looked crestfallen. He'd picked the winner and then failed to act on his own extrasensory impulse. He moved his jawbone around as if he'd just taken a punch to the chin, and his colleague laughed again, this time with feeling.

For those with a casual interest in horseracing, it's disappointing to find out how technical most racing news is. Everyday coverage focuses almost exclusively on statistics. The *Daily Racing Form*, the bettor's Bible, is full of past-performance records that supply a deluge of data on individual horses – split times, medication history, trainer records, race conditions, workout times, lifetime earnings. Articles interpret the data, and the writing there is no-nonsense, business-page stuff.

But despite all the statistics in the papers, you can still make out the outlines of a larger story: humans encourage (beg, implore) horses to win; horses insist on their stubborn unpredictability. Tipsheets are rich in the poignant and familiar shorthand of failure. Race records carry a single line of description for every outing, and these read like the hasty journal entries you might scribble down at the end of a bad day: 'set pace, tired'; 'stalked, lacked rally'; 'dwelled, drew even, edged late'; 'failed to menace'; 'broke in tangle'; 'faltered'; 'showed nothing'.

Over the Breeders' Cup weekend, three separate people told me the story of Zippy Chippy, a nine-year-old gelding who'd lost a record eighty-eight outings, and was now banned from most tracks because he was dangerously slow out of the gates. But his owner, Felix Monserrate, loved Zippy and entered him in any contest he could find. He even had him race a man – Jose Herrera, a center fielder for the Rochester Red Wings, a farm team for the Baltimore Orioles. The man beat the horse. 'Forty yards is not enough for Zippy to get warm,' Monserrate said. 'He let Jose win to make him feel good.'

It's easy to find this sort of insouciance at the track. During the Juvenile race, for two-year-old colts, three women standing along the rail at the owners' Skye Terrace whooped so passionately midway through the running that the final results seemed beside the point. A silver-haired fellow in tweeds came up to them after the finish to see how they did.

'Did you win?'

'We did,' one of them answered. 'Until they kep' on going.'

All day long, the favorites kept lumbering across the finish line at the back of the pack. Horses under contract to Coolmore Stud had an especially slow day: A. P. Valentine, a promising two-year-old whose stud rights Magnier had shelled out $14 million for, came in last; Fusaichi Pegasus, who'd cost him $60 million, came in sixth. Meanwhile, the long shots leaped to the front and stayed there: the 56–1 Spain was joined by the 47–1 Caressing, and in the day's biggest race, the $4 million Classic, Tiznow, a California-bred horse (the owners had to pay a $360,000 late-entry fee twenty days before the race) beat Coolmore's son of Storm Cat, Giant's Causeway, by a neck. (The Cal-bred Tiznow repeated the feat in the 2001 Breeders' Cup Classic, edging out Sheikh Mohammed's Sakhee in a photo finish.)

Down by the paddock, where the jockeys jumped up onto saddles the size of soap slivers, the bettors cursed amiably and pushed toward the rail to watch the horses parading by. They hoped to detect the type of spark that doesn't show up in racing-form statistics – a bargain horse dancing on his toes or staring down the favorite – but after a few races, they pretty much abandoned the pretense of study. 'Hell nation,' one man said, 'I'm sharp as a bowling ball today.'

'I'd like to know what these guys are giving these suckers. I want to have some of it myself.'

A woman in black velvet boots stuck her sunglasses down her cleavage and told her date, 'I can't keep supporting your betting habits.' Strangely, people's moods were as light as their pockets – maybe it was the julep line at the Churchill Downs concession stands, but there was a powerful sense of futility, too, and rising against it you could feel the blend of grim humor and random friendliness that you often find among people stranded together by natural disaster.

Down at the food court closest to the finish line, there was a bank of closed-circuit televisions – a great spot to watch people watching the race. Smokers and last-minute bettors packed together in the space between pillars. An Englishman rolled up his program and slapped his own hand, hard, as if whipping his horse down the stretch. Everybody yelled. Jock fans yelled the names of their favorites ('Come on, Chavez. Come on, Chop-Chop'). You could hear numbers and nicknames shouted at the horses on TV and in the middle of it all, a blond guy with an earring, dressed in black everything, sat in his wheelchair, watching the screens. Over the course of two races, he never moved or varied his expression once.

After Tiznow, wearing number 13, won the Classic, his jockey, Chris McCarron, in hot-pink silks with blue polka dots, thanked the owners, Michael Cooper and Cecilia Straub-Rubens, for putting up the $360,000 it took to run in the race. 'That's gamesmanship,' he said. But gamesmanship was only half the story.

McCarron could have called it recklessness or clairvoyance, too. Mrs Straub-Rubens, a statuesque eighty-three-year-old in pink-tinted glasses and Lady Bird Johnson hairdo, accepted the championship trophy from the Kentucky governor. The sun had come out again, just in time for a presentation photo in the November sunset, and Straub-Rubens smiled a pretty, closed-lip smile for the press. Three days later, she died.

FOUR

The Little Baldhead Guy and the Black Guy

I F YOU WANT TO buy a horse, you could spend hours studying the pedigree charts and looking up the race records of a yearling's sire and dam and grandam, hunting for evidence of overlooked reserves of speed or staying power. Or you could just ask somebody who was there. The day after the Breeders' Cup, I went to Keeneland to tour the sales grounds with the seventy-five-year-old veterinarian Robert Copelan, who helps Overbrook decide which horses to bid hundreds of thousands of dollars on. Dr Copelan is an experienced judge of horseflesh. He was a racetrack vet, at Beulah Park, Thistledown, Churchill Downs, and Arlington, among others, for forty-eight years. By now, he can take one look at a weanling or yearling with a certain type of knee or set to the shoulder or hitch in the step and tell you the problems that horse will develop when he or she really runs. At the track, he said, he specialized in 'unsoundness of wind and limb'. And Copelan knows which of these problems can be fixed, because every weekend from 1963 to 2000, he operated on horses at his own veterinary hospital, Sunnyside Surgery. The name fits his disposition, although so would a place called Talks-a-Lot.

Partly, he talks because talking is his job. A few times a week, he tours the Overbrook barns with a microcassette, assessing the conformation of every foal and yearling ('Good muscular development without being overdone – he's not like Charles Atlas. He's a very tidy little guy who's put up well in front'). Transcripts of his character studies help the farm identify the best racing prospects early and speed their development. He has the breeder's habit of referring to horses by their parents ('She's a fair representation of a Foolish Pleasure'). Since he retired from surgery, in 2000, his intimate knowledge of the vices and virtues of the principal families of Thoroughbred horses is perhaps his most salable asset.

But he also talks because he's good at it. As he walked through the Keeneland barns, people stopped him – to tell him a dirty joke, to ask him to scope a horse they might buy, to talk about the Derby-winning trainer who committed suicide, to verify the right medication to settle a yearling's cough. He introduced me to the brother of a Triple Crown–winning jockey, to a friend of his who went deaf when they were both in elementary school, to a guy who saves parking spots for working vets, and to the fellow who'd trained the colt that the great owner Fred W. Hooper named after him. (About the honor, Copelan says: 'I saw my own obit in the *Racing Form* a few years ago: "Copelan Dies at 17." ') When he wasn't talking, he walked from one barn to the next with an almost comical speed – a bantamweight blur in a big down coat that made him easy to spot. Still, no matter how fast he was going, if he stopped to talk, all his hurry disappeared.

At most jobs, a guy his age would be old. But in the breeding business, the energy and innovation of youth are far less valuable than the patience and perspective that comes from seeing fifty crops of three-year-olds hit the track. And the chances are good that, somewhere along the sireline, Copelan paid a visit. As a seventeen-year-old exercise boy, he galloped horses at Beulah Park. He broke Hill Gail, the 1952 Kentucky Derby winner, as a yearling at Calumet. He may not be right when he casually states that the greatest crop of three-year-olds ever was the class of 1957 – he quickly cites Iron Liege, Bold Ruler, Gallant Man, Round Table, Federal Hill – but it would be hard to find somebody better qualified to argue the point.

It's easy to get the impression, as you follow him and his fifty-one-year-old assistant, Randy Speakes, on the day after the Breeders' Cup, that they're every bit as serious about joking with each other as they are about seeing all the yearlings on their list. ('I've worked with him for twenty-seven years, and we get along like brothers,' Speakes says. 'And that's just why I bother coming to work – because I know that I can fuck with him all the time.') Still, like any old dance partners, the pair have their favorite routines, and over the course of the day they keep returning to two apparently unserious themes to pass the time. One of them is Copelan's houseguests, who seem to be giving him an incentive to stay out in the barns and work longer.

'But if you say anything about that,' he warns one man he confessed this to, 'I'll tell I seen you with a colored girl.'

We're standing around a shedrow whose working population is fairly evenly divided between black and white attendants – the reader should remember that the speaker is a devilish little seventy-five-year-old whose natural expression is a likable smirk. Speakes, who is black, turns to me and says, 'You know, some colored girls can look good.'

Speakes – everyone calls him Randy and calls Copelan Doc – has a high tenor voice, a spry and skinny frame, and a long-suffering nature. The music of his accent seems out of date, like a railway porter's in an RKO picture. Even though he's fifty-one, he handles the athletic requirements of the job casually, balancing on the bottom half of a stall door to reach an electric outlet or grabbing a handful of an unruly horse to steady her while Doc performs a routine examination. He keeps track of things he knows Doc tends not to pay attention to, and he drops in and out of the steady conversation, hanging back when Doc starts offering veterinary advice and jumping in again when it's time to pack up and go to the next barn.

As they hopscotch across the sales ground, the other theme they keep returning to is Speakes's frequent appearances in *Indian Charlie*, a single sheet of prank news items and horse ads written by Eddie Musselman in a folksy, g-droppin' style, and handed out free at the sales by a leggy stunner dressed in zebra pants or black catsuits with boa ruffs, etc. In his tout sheet, Musselman invariably refers to Speakes as Randy Copelan: according to the paper, Speakes is the result of the mating of Doc Copelan and Aretha Franklin. During the September sales, this Randy Copelan figure was one of a dozen characters in *Indian Charlie*'s serialized version of *Survivor*. Each day, the lead item chronicled the adventures (and sequential casting out) of twelve prominent figures in the breeding world – W. T. Young, Will Farish, Sheikh Mohammed, D. Wayne Lukas, Randy Copelan, and so on – marooned together in fictional seclusion in The Castle. (The Castle is an absurd but entirely real place just west of Keeneland, with twelve turrets, a crenellated outer wall, a drawbridge, and the makings of a moat; just before construction was complete, the wife of the man who built it sued for divorce.)

'Randy Copelan' survived six installments, only to end up getting kicked out because he broke into a first-aid kit equipped with 'Colt 45 Malt Liquor and Mad Dog 20–20 vine, a fifth of gin and a pickle jar full of Alphabet Jones' Grade-A moonshine corn liquor, bottled in 1999'. He didn't stop sampling the contents 'until he'd cured himself of every disease known to man, and 4 or 5 others that ain't been discovered yet'. When Sheikh Mohammed objected to the smell of alcohol on Randy's breath, *Indian Charlie* had Randy deliver the unlikely retort 'Kiss my ass, Camel boy'.

As we make our way down the hill from Barn 49 toward the

parking lot, Doc explains, 'They said Randy'd got into the Mad Dog 20–20 and he knew a lot about mixing it because he'd been with his daddy for so many years.'

'What did Mr Young get thowed out for?' Speakes asks.

'He didn't bother anybody, but he took an economy-size jar of peanut butter.'

'And he went out in the woods with it.'

'And what did he say about Mary Jean Wall and Helen Alexander?' Doc asks, about two highly connected women of breeding, the turf writer for the Lexington *Herald-Leader* and the owner of Middlebrook Farm, respectively.

'They were having a brassiere-snapping bitch fight.'

The two of them seem to enjoy reviewing the satire. They assure me that the enjoyment was nearly universal: all the people who left the sales early, Speakes says, wanted copies faxed to them to find out how it ended.

As we walk along the sweetgum trees between the barns, a silver-haired man with a wandering eye and a black dog at his boots calls out, 'Hey, Doc, how you doing?'

We sidle up to the wooden fence outside the enclosure where John Williams, the onetime farm manager at Spendthrift, is keeping his consignment. Speakes looks down at the dog, a Lab so pitch black that Williams named him Angus, and says, 'That dog's like me, because we both so dark.'

Williams chooses to ignore this comment. He's in a sunny mood, and Copelan seems to recognize the symptoms he's presenting – Williams clearly has a horse in his barn that both Magnier and the Sheikh are interested in – so he says, 'You selling Caress?'

'She's right here,' he answers, and if Williams made a gesture, I missed it. A tall woman comes by offering apples – green Harrisons all the way from Minnesota, we're told – and just as we each take one, a dark bay broodmare on a short lead walks over. She's heavily pregnant – she looks as if she's hiding a pyramid – and from the way she takes possession of the spit of gravel, you can tell it's the end of her day and she's in no mood for messing around.

Williams mentions that she's by Storm Cat. 'He's the predominant sire right now,' he adds, just filling the air while Copelan looks her over. 'He had a horse running yesterday I was very impressed with.'

'Giant's Causeway?' Copelan asks.

'He's something.'

'So's the winner.'

'It was a good race.'

Speakes is already halfway through his apple. 'These are good,' he says, between bites.

'Harrisons, they call them?' Doc asks. 'Oh, boy, well, I'm going to try one.' He doesn't. He keeps circling the horse slowly, like a teenager checking out a muscle car. He drops one understatement ('Well, this is a pretty one') before finally coming back around her haunches to ask, 'Did we breed this mare?'

Caress was born in 1991, which means she was conceived in the breeding season of 1990. That was Storm Cat's third year at stud and the nadir of his popularity. For the second straight season, Overbrook had reduced his stud fee; the farm was cutting deals right and left. 'Here's how it happened,' Williams says. 'We said let's do a foal share, do a two-year deal. The deal was we'd get one and Mr Young gets one. And I got to pick the first. So this one was born and I said to Lou, "Look, I don't know what the next one's going to look like but this is a nice horse. Let's go ahead and take it." So I called and said, "We'll take that one, you get the next one." This is Caress and the next one was Country Cat. We both win.'

'We both won, didn't we?'

Copelan suddenly remembers Country Cat ('looked like Quasimodo, but she could run like hell') but much of the conversation between the two men is inscrutable, carried on in racing-fanatic shorthand ('She was something in the Acorn. This mare here wasn't something in a Grade I') so detailed that I have to spend several days checking my notes against the race records of the two fillies to make out what they're saying. Every once in a while, they return to speaking English: 'She's really the deal, ain't she?'

'She's got quality all over her.'

Through it all, they sound as amiable as a couple of Shriners talking about each other's grandkids. You could walk by and not think a thing of it, except that this sort of give-and-take – a couple of old horsemen chatting about a horse or two around a paddock fence – is what due diligence sounds like in the horse business. In this case, the amusing details all relate, ultimately, to Storm Cat. Both men have profited over the past ten years as the Overbrook stallion climbed the sire lists. Copelan profited because, the first year Storm Cat went to stud, W. T. Young gave him a lifetime breeding right (the right to send one mare to Storm Cat or sell that service, every year, for as long as the horse shall stand). And Williams – well, he's got a mare he didn't pay a cent to breed who is about to sell for seven figures. (Williams's excitement is justified. Two days after this encounter, Caress sells for $3.1 million to Sheikh Mohammed.)

Finally, Williams can restrain himself no longer. 'Doc,' he says, 'one cover every year!' This is one of the most amusing idiosyncrasies of the breeding industry: the intimate details of procreation keep showing up in sales pitches and advertisements. A big banner at the Breeders' Cup, for instance, proclaimed 'Giant's Causeway: Sold in Utero by Taylor Made!' And Williams, with his 'one cover every year', is boasting that Caress is so fertile that she needs only one trip to the breeding shed to conceive. This is a double recommendation, because it indicates her impeccable reproductive fitness, and because, if she always gets pregnant on her first heat of the season, it means she's more likely to have an early, and hence stronger and more salable, foal.

Williams seems a little chagrined by his own outburst. 'I wasn't trying to sell her, Bob.'

'Yeah, I know it.'

'She's a beautiful filly.'

'Everything about her is just class,' Copelan says. He turns to Speakes. 'You got the apples?'

'They good.'

Back in Spendthrift's heyday (as one Lexingtonian put it, 'back before drunk driving became such a big issue'), the folks selling horses used to push bourbon on their customers, not apples. Williams warns them about the sourness of the apples, but he does so with such a curious image ('You can suck up an eighteen-gauge needle after you finish that') that conversation stops and we are left to contemplate a vision of Williams vigorously engaged in some sort of activity involving forceful sucking and veterinary implements.

'I know what you're saying,' Doc says at last, and by the time he walks through the gate, he's wearing his usual sly, suggestive grin. 'Well, I've got a lot of secrets.'

This makes the three men laugh and hoot. I recognize from the cackling heartiness of the laughter, and the way it's quickly followed by conspiratorial banter over the gate, that they're taking leave of each other with a little recreational raunchiness. But I can't tell what particular sexual act they're being so secretive about until Williams quotes some friend of theirs who liked to boast about 'eating pussy before it became fashionable'.

Doc suggests a better phrase: 'Tell him to say, "when it was a disgrace".' I like imagining the era they're evoking – a sort of pre-feminist dawn of enlightened pussy-eating connoisseurship – and I like the way these old Kentucky hardboots modestly avoid any boasting while managing to suggest that they played a pivotal role in the advancement of the art.

'He keeps me around,' Speakes says, 'because I know the best secret.'

'And niggers lie about it,' Doc confides to Williams. Doc drops the 'nigger' so naturally into the conversation, you could almost miss it. It seems easy in the saying – whether out of habit, or permission, or presumption of intimacy – and the laughter that follows it looks relaxed and unexceptional. Somehow Doc's comment leads to bawdy joking about Mike Tyson's rape conviction and more rounds of hearty and mutual guffawing.

When they all recover, Speakes points at me and says, 'You embarrass the man.'

It's hard to tell what Speakes thinks I'm embarrassed by – the casual use of the word 'nigger' by a white man in the presence of his black employee, the casual use of the word 'pussy' in the presence of a pregnant mare, or the fixation on the sexual habits of a rapist – but before I've figured it out, the conversation with Williams quickly ends and Doc hustles away.

The next day I follow the two men again. Doc is as energetic and patient as ever, pulling me aside after he rejects a horse, to point out what he didn't like (a straight shoulder, 'which means that she doesn't have the ability to diffuse concussive forces when she goes at high speeds'). At one point, Speakes, too, pulls me aside, to tell me how generous Doc is with his time, and it's obvious how much the two men like and depend on each other. After one episode in a stall, pulling out the three-foot endoscope and peeking down the lungs of a yearling, Speakes starts packing up the equipment. He turns to Doc and schemingly announces: 'I'll tell you what we're going to do. Now we done already did this. We're going to put this away.' He points to the twenty-thousand-dollar instrument and its padded carrying case – 'See, I'm going to unplug it. Then I'll put it away.'

'Yes, Dolph,' Doc says (using his nickname for Randolph Speakes). 'That ain't any different than we always do.' Doc laughs, clearly enjoying himself. He turns to me. 'I'm standing here listening. I thought he had some kind of plan.'

Once he sees that he had Doc going, Speakes laughs, too. He says, 'Kevin will go back home and he'll say, "You know, I met this little baldhead guy and this black guy . . . "'

Doc finishes his sentence, taking on the exaggerated drawl you'd expect to hear from somebody reading an Uncle Remus story. 'And the black guy was the cause of a-a-a-all of his troubles.'

FIVE

Triple Crown Winner in Winter

I T ' S J A N U A R Y , C O L D F O R Kentucky and as bright as it gets on a day with no sun. Last week's heavy snow has mostly melted or blown off, and the pasture at Three Chimneys Farm, on Old Frankfort Pike, is a patchy, faded orange, the color of an old lion. Seattle Slew, the winner of the Triple Crown as a three-year-old in 1977, is twenty-seven now, and he's enduring his afternoon physical-therapy session – a half-mile walk, down the hill and back. He's recovering from an emergency spinal fusion, a surgery never before attempted on a horse his age. Right now, half a mile, twice a day, is as far as he's allowed to go. Tom Wade, his groom for the past sixteen years, walks silently beside him, and Karen and Mickey Taylor, his owners, trail behind. Karen is filming the trip, as she does every day, to send to Slew's surgeon. Mickey is talking about how smart Slew is.

'His intelligence is unbelievable,' Mickey says. Mickey wears ostrich-skin cowboy boots, a couple layers of sweatshirt and parkas, and a baseball cap that says SLEW O'GOLD. That's the name of one of Seattle Slew's sons, but it also describes the fairytale amounts of money that Slew has brought in over the years. When the Taylors bought him – for $17,500 – in 1975, Mickey was a logger and Karen a stewardess, and they lived in a mobile home in White Swan, Washington. Ten years later, in 1985, Seattle Slew was said to be worth more than the Pan Am Building, which was what the fifty-nine-story Met Life Building over Grand Central Station was called back then.

'A lot of horses are intelligent,' Karen says. 'But Slew —'

'He's a different level.'

'He loves mud, too,' Karen adds.

Horse people often talk like this, but the claims they make about the intelligence of horses don't seem all that extravagant in human terms. According to Tom Wade, Slew knows not to eat plants he's never seen before. And Mickey tells me that after the spinal fusion, when Slew couldn't turn his neck to bite his itches, he found something in his stall to rub against instead. At first, the testimonials don't seem like much, but people keep offering them, and it starts to add up: If a mare kicks, Mickey tells me, Slew walks right out of the breeding shed and won't have anything more to do with her. Also, Slew can take one look and tell whether a mare's in heat — if she's not, he won't bother. One vet saw Slew walk away from a mare that he had certified as ready to breed, and the vet was dumb enough to say, 'You want to tell me that stallion is smarter than me?'

On this chilly day, however, you're less likely to be impressed by Slew's intellectual accomplishments than by his furriness, currently highlighted by quills of dried yellow dirt caked on his hindquarters, the proud evidence of his last roll in the mud. 'He's got more hair than these young bucks,' Wade says, gesturing dismissively at the rest of the stallions enjoying the chill and fly-free January climate in the Three Chimneys paddocks. Wade, a no-nonsense forty-three-year-old of equal parts heft and unhurried dignity, left school at sixteen to 'rub horses'. A few years ago, after the horse-crazy British monarch, Elizabeth II, sought an audience with the Triple Crown winner, Wade had the chance to give his mother a photograph of 'Seattle Slew, Tom, and the Queen of England'. His mother hung it up in her beauty shop.

When we get to the bottom of the hill, Wade and Slew turn

around and start back up the hill. As they pass us by, Mickey Taylor says, 'How are you, Fuzzy-Wuzzy?' Slew seems preoccupied and pays him no mind.

Halfway up the rise, a gray horse runs alertly to his paddock fence, then beats a sheepish retreat – Silver Charm, who won the Kentucky Derby and Preakness in 1997, and the Dubai World Cup in 1998. He's a horse who should be in the movies, a real looker with dark gray stockings and a silvery moonscape across his haunches. When he showed up at the farm a year ago, he was the year's prize stallion – a fierce battler who fell one stride short of the Triple Crown himself. Everyone wanted to breed to him. Slew had other ideas.

'When he first came here,' Taylor says, chuckling, 'Slew thought it was a gray mare. He loves gray mares.' But as soon as the savvy stud cleared up that misconception, there were other matters to settle. One morning, Slew left his stall for his regular jog – this was before the onset of his spinal problems, when he still ran a brisk mile a day with Three Chimneys' exercise rider – and Silver Charm was ready, a stallion recruit standing at the bars of his stall, waiting to take on the old hoss. A stall away, Capote, another son of Seattle Slew, was bobbing and weaving nervously. Slew walked first to Capote, and he stood there in silence till his son quit dancing. 'And then he went over,' Mickey says, 'and him and Silver Charm just locked, boom, eye to eye. And the exercise rider was right there watching. And they stayed, you know, locked right on, until all at once Silver Charm turned his head and went to the back of the stall. And from then on, that was the routine every morning. When Slew came out, Capote would look at him, quit bobbing and weaving, and Silver Charm would go hide in the back. It's funny, the pecking order.'

As far as Slew is concerned, all that was decided long ago. He passes Silver Charm's paddock without a glance, concentrating instead on the task of walking. Slew walks carefully now – not ploddingly, like a cart horse, just carefully, as if he doesn't quite trust his footing and he'd rather watch the grass and the hill and the crushed brick paths under his hooves than deal with any of the profounder implications of his plight. Like so many afflictions that can bring down a horse, his came on suddenly. On the morning of January 13, almost one month before the beginning of breeding season, the exercise rider came back from the morning run and told Wade that Slew was 'going a little bit funny behind'. Wade kept an eye on him and, sure enough, a couple hours later, Slew's hind-quarters fell completely out of alignment. To go forward, the only undefeated winner of the Triple Crown had to scramble sideways like a crab.

Wade jumped into the stall and held Slew steady, maneuvering him to the cinder-block wall and pushing him against it until the horse could feel his groom's heft compensating for the instability in his own stance. It's another mark of Slew's intelligence that he chose to trust his groom just then, that faced with calamity he didn't give in to the instinct for panic and break into a spastic but still powerful attempt at flight that could easily have killed him. Tom Wade leaned into Slew's hindquarters, and as he did, he felt the horse's breath slowly steadying. He called for help, and the two of them, Wade and Slew, waited for it to come.

Wade will deny it (he says this story is about 'the dedication of people that give their lives to go to school to take care of animals'), but none of the high-tech heroism that followed – the steady handiwork of teams of surgeons, radiologists, and anesthesiologists; their cool professionalism in the face of huge financial risk and professional humiliation – none of it would have been possible without Tom Wade's first timely intervention. And, of course, that only happened because Seattle Slew let it happen. Trust is selective, even capricious – this is just as true for horses as it is for people. But Slew was smart enough not only to choose trust over panic in the first place, but to know the right man to trust in a crisis.

The old stud walks to the hilltop now where the farm has set up a portable fifty-foot pen. It's large enough to give him a sense of freedom but not so big that he gets any illusions about running around, prepping for the Kentucky Derby. Wade leads Slew in and shuts the gate, and the horse grazes a little, scratches his coat against the metal wires, then falls to his knees and rolls on his back with the sort of blissful little shudder you hear from an old man getting into a hot bath.

Karen Taylor keeps filming, and Mickey wanders over to the Airstream trailer they had shipped onto the farm – except for one weekend when they flew to Santa Anita to watch a stakes race, the Taylors have shown up every day for the past year, to film, to hand-feed Slew his favorite Washington apples and carrots, to mix his medicine into the Gerber's that the horse finds palatable. ('How big is your baby?' the checkout girl asked, when Mickey came through with his second case of mashed carrots in a week. 'Twelve hundred and sixty pounds,' he said.)

The Taylors have no children – Karen suffered a miscarriage after Slew's Triple Crown campaign – and no matter how much they've gained from his efforts at the track and in the breeding shed (a house in Ketchum, Idaho; a horse farm in Hagerman, Idaho; another place in Yakima, Washington) no one who watches their fretful parental puttering around Slew could ever accuse them of placing their own financial interests ahead of Slew's welfare, putting him through radical surgery just to squeeze one more breeding season out of the golden horse.

Karen and Mickey love talking about Slew, and they have the habit, common among horsemen, of lapsing indiscriminately into the first person when discussing his racing career. They'll say, 'when *we* won the Champagne' (about the Champagne Stakes, the highlight of the two-year-old racing season, which Slew won in record time), or 'when *we* got roughed up in the gate' (in the Kentucky Derby, when

Slew broke slowly and still won by a comfortable margin). Sometimes, they'll skip the collective and just speak on Slew's behalf: 'He's so athletic that he thinks, *Well, hell, I'll just go faster*' (about Slew's ill-advised attempts to out*run* his neurological problems).

But their most unlikely use of the first person came when Mickey returned from the Taylors' Airstream with a copy of a letter from a Texan 'equine reproductive consultant'. The letter okayed Slew's return to the breeding shed and, on the basis of four 'collection procedures' and subsequent microscopic analysis of the longevity and motility of his sperm, certified his renewed fertility. According to Taylor, Slew had always been tremendously fertile: 'He's the only horse in Kentucky that can get mares in foal across a fence' is the way he put it. But a few months after the neurological problems began on January 13, 2000 (as Wade says, after the horse got 'all cocked over in the rear end'), Slew's legendary potency deserted him. His stud career appeared to be over, and the Taylors, the vets, and the Three Chimneys brass decided to pull him from the stallion roster and undertake the risky spinal operation, in hopes of rewarding the stallion with the healthy retirement he richly deserved.

But now Mickey was waving a letter claiming that Seattle Slew had recovered from what the consultant referred to as a 'transient testicular insult'. In the interests of thoroughness, the man had taken calipers to measure the width and length of the recently insulted pair ('Note,' the consultant warned, 'this measurement might not be accurate, as Seattle Slew kept retracting his testis high into the scrotum and objected to pulling it down for measurement of length'). Mickey chatted with me about seasonal swelling – stallions, it seems, have a larger 'testicular volume' during the breeding season – and he pointed out a few measurements that showed a resiliency in Slew of which Mickey seemed unusually proud, figures that proved that the horse, even in the chill of January, was still hanging out in midseason form. But apparently the earlier shrinkage – the original insult – still weighed heavily; Mickey knew all of Slew's measurements, before and after, as if they were his own. 'Here,' he said. 'See? Our testicles went down. This went down to sixty, and this went down to a hundred and ten . . .'

Seattle Slew has always been cast as the workingman's Triple Crown winner, an arriviste who followed too closely on the heels of the hero Secretariat, and too many people in racing circles thought Slew's Triple Crown campaign cheapened the earlier emphatic achievement. When Secretariat won the same trio of races four years earlier, he came across as a blueblood, stepping into the winner's circle escorted by his owner, the Virginia grand dame Penny Chenery Tweedy, 'the first lady of American racing' according to the Nixon-era lionizers. Slew, on the other hand, showed up with a vet, the vet's wife, a logger, and a stewardess. This slaphappy quartet of owners (the Taylors owned Slew with another couple, the vet Jim Hill and his wife, Sandy) looked like cast members of *Love, American Style*. They wore SLEW CREW T-shirts around the shedrows, as if dressed for a Thursday-night bowling league.

A quick skim through the pedigrees tends to confirm this class-conscious casting. Secretariat's sire and dam were Bold Ruler and Something Royal; earlier generations included such regal namesakes as Princequillo, Imperatrice, Pompey, and Cleopatra. Slew's sire was Bold Reasoning, a second-generation Bold Ruler knockoff; his dam was My Charmer, by Poker; and you can make out this same hard-knocks combination of ballsiness and guile in such forebears as Reason to Earn, Fair Charmer, Glamour, and Jet Pilot.

The horses looked their parts. Secretariat was a beautiful chestnut-red, distinctively marked with three high white stockings and a star. Slew, on the other hand, was dark brown, with no distinguishing marks other than muscle. Their racing styles, too, were opposites. Secretariat entered races as the favorite and won with a sort of charismatic contempt, by inarguable margins in record times. He won the Belmont Stakes by thirty-one lengths after his greatest rival, Sham – whose second-place clocking in the Kentucky Derby was faster than any other horse's winning time before or since – gave up after six furlongs, so thoroughly beaten that he never raced again.

Slew, however, relied on dangerous bursts of speed, which he deployed like a pool hustler: enough to win, but not so much that he scared off all the money. This is not to say that he didn't win handily, too – in the Champagne, he crossed the finish line nearly ten lengths ahead of the second-place horse. It was just that you could never be sure how much he had left, and this dark-horse reserve could seem troublesome, unsettling. People generally prefer heroes with nothing to hide, like Secretariat, whose runaway victory in the Belmont looked like an act of noblesse oblige: if the other horses couldn't match him that day, he was prepared to race all out anyway, for history, for the record books, for the crowds. Secretariat thrived in the limelight – Chenery said that long after he left the track, throughout his sixteen years at Claiborne Farm, he would always prick up his ears when he heard the click of a camera, and would pose, gazing regally into the distance. But Slew was not so accommodating, and the old racetrack habit that *he* hung on to could hardly be interpreted as the gesture of a publicity seeker: when visitors came to his stall, Slew offered his backside and refused to budge.

He never pretended to be knowable, and maybe that's why there's far less talk about his many cagey victories than about his photo-finish loss, in 1978, at Belmont Park, to Exceller in the Jockey Club Gold Cup. Exceller was a fine horse that Slew had beaten before. It was near the end of his four-year-old season, after Slew had trounced Affirmed, the third Triple Crown winner of the 1970s, in a race he led from start to finish. Five weeks later, the two champions faced each other again, and again Slew broke out of the gate in first. The three-year-old Affirmed ran, as he often did, with his own pacesetter, Life's Hope, and the pair tried to challenge Slew for the early lead. But Slew held them off, and after a mile the relay efforts of the two stablemates faded. At this point, Exceller began his move from thirty lengths behind the speedsters, but when he drew even, Slew still wasn't done. He found a second burst of speed – most horses are lucky to have one – and he matched the fresher horse, stride for stride, to the photo finish. It was the one race where he showed the world what track hands call his heart.

Of course, all horses are unknowable – this is one of their attractions – but Slew was not only unknowable, he made no effort to be nice about it. The combination gave him a prickly, Miles Davis cool, and as is so often the case when you're hanging out with the cool, there were a lot of rules. Slew had to be fed first, trained first, bred first. You did not walk in front of him. You did not, under any circumstances, enter his paddock. You did not talk about him behind his back.

After one of Slew's three losses, his jockey, Jean Cruguet, bitched to the press about him: 'I told those people he wasn't ready for the race after beating four bums going seven furlongs. I told them he wouldn't beat Dr Patches.' Cruguet never rode Slew again.

The jockey who replaced him, Angel Cordero, had been begging for the ride for nearly two years, ever since Slew beat his horse, For the Moment, in the Champagne Stakes. Cordero and his mounts had lost to Slew on many occasions, so he was familiar with Slew's intimidating style, the way he stared down not just the horse but the rider as well. Cordero, who was not beyond using intimidation tactics himself, couldn't help admiring this cold and level eye. He told a reporter that as Slew pulled away from him in the Kentucky Derby, he said, 'Good-bye, soul brother.'

But Cordero was unprepared for Slew's intensity of focus. He knew all about his pre-race 'war dance', the way Slew kept his legs constantly churning from the moment he came out of the tunnel. But he was surprised to find that as soon as they entered the starting gate, all the footwork stopped and Slew froze in place and began taking tremendously deep and steady breaths. Cordero told the Taylors that in eighteen years of riding – on more than twenty thousand horses – he'd never seen anything like it. He'd seen horses go crazy, bucking and savaging the boys in the starting gates. He'd seen one horse simply lie down. But he'd never seen a horse 'blow up' like that, drawing breaths so deep that the barrel of his chest seemed to double in size. The veins on his neck stood out and Seattle Slew stared directly ahead, waiting for the gates to open, waiting to run.

These days, though, Slew's racing was over, and he was waiting to breed.

SIX

The Old Stud Returns

THE EUREKA MOMENT: early 1977, the Frontier Lounge, Las Vegas. Onstage, Bobbie Gentry, ten years removed from her Grammy for 'Ode to Billie Joe', and Larry Storch, equally far from his role as Corporal Randolph Agarn on *F Troop*. In the audience, two vets, Barrie Grant and Pamela Wagner, and one doctor of human medicine, an orthopedic surgeon, George Bagby, all down from Washington State University for an orthopedic surgery convention. In the Vegas glow, the two ambitious vets and the pioneering surgeon didn't talk about the faded stars. They talked about the latest spinal fusion technique (called the Cloward technique and designed to help relieve disorders caused by spinal compression) and whether it could work with horses just as well as it was working with humans.

The Cloward technique had junked all the plates and screws that made spinal fusion surgery so cumbersome and gave postsurgical X rays the look of a messy tool drawer. With the new technique, a hole was drilled between vertebrae and a hollow cylinder was tamped into the hole, purposely drilled a millimeter or so too small. (In the original surgeries, the cylinder was made of bone taken from a bone bank or from the iliac crest on the patient's pelvis; some years later, Bagby fashioned a cylinder, now called the Bagby basket, out of stainless steel.) The small difference in size did the trick – once the oversize cylinder was jammed in place, the resulting pressure fused the new bone and two vertebrae together. The pioneering vets wanted to find out if the procedure had become so efficient that they could try it on horses.

The first horse that Grant and Wagner tried to fit with this bone dowel died four days after surgery. It was a mildly encouraging outcome, to everyone but the horse, and the team felt confident enough to make the second surgery a demonstration procedure, at a type of professional open house, on Saturday morning, May 7, 1977. Dr Bagby scrubbed in, and under his guidance the surgery went off perfectly, in under two hours. While the horse, Finelli, slowly came to in the recovery room, Grant rushed home – to watch Seattle Slew win the Kentucky Derby – then hurried back, just in time to see his patient rise gamely to his feet.

Finelli survived and prospered, but it wasn't until September that Grant actually witnessed the extent of his recovery. The colt came in for emergency sutures on a cut, a deep wound that required ten days of stall rest. Grant paid special attention to the way the three-year-old moved at his first taste of freedom: when he was finally led out to a hilly paddock behind the clinic, Finelli raced to the crest of the hill and back down, bucking and turning and kicking along the way, in an impressively reckless indulgence in the pleasures of speed. Grant remembers saying to himself, 'Geez, this horse got better.'

In the years since, with practice and technical improvement, the surgery had changed, although it was generally seen as a last-ditch measure to be attempted only on young horses, like Finelli, who suffered from what textbook writers call equine spinal ataxia or cervical vertebral malformation and everyone else calls wobbles, because that's what the poor horse does.

There were several reasons why older horses didn't undergo the surgery. It was riskier, because their bones were more brittle. There was, too, the economic reality: few older horses were worth the expense – around four to six thousand dollars for the surgery itself, and even more for the fairly constant care and physical therapy that the horse would require in the months afterwards. And, according to Grant, 'there's still some belief in the horse industry that you can't do anything about a horse with spinal-cord compression. And then why put a nice old horse through that stuff when he's already paid his dues?'

But Three Chimneys didn't operate like that. The place looks reassuringly traditional – if it weren't a horse farm, you'd be happy sending your only daughter there – but the management has always been comfortable doing things a little differently. They have a woman, Sandy Hatfield, in charge of the stallions. The owner, Robert Clay, is from an old Kentucky family, out of the sireline of Cassius Clay, the emancipationist who freed Muhammad Ali's great-grandmother. He's kept Three Chimneys going with a mixture of unconventional horsemanship (the practice of galloping stallions is apparently unique to the farm) and misleadingly modest business strategy: it was Clay's idea that stallion owners might prefer a small boutique operation instead of the big 'horse factories', and in 1985, at the peak of the Bluegrass Bubble, when Gainesway was juggling forty-two stallions and Spendthrift thirty-five, Clay quietly began advertising a place where a few handpicked sires would get plenty of individual attention.

In January 2000, individual attention was exactly what Seattle Slew required. Thankfully, the Three Chimneys vet, Dr Jim More-head, a big Missourian with the sort of rough good looks – square jaw, blue eyes, pushbroom mustache – that fit perfectly on a Super Bowl coach, or an airline pilot, or, apparently, a vet, seemed to welcome the challenge. He started off conservatively, giving Slew bute (the common antiinflammatory phenylbutazone, a sort of equine aspirin that Slew had had a good response to at the track) and Banamine (another antiinflammatory). He called in specialists, who took ultrasound and radiographic images of his spine. The images seemed to suggest arthritic bone growth impinging on the nerves. But there was a problem: Seattle Slew was a twenty-six-year-old stallion, and, Morehead said, 'We had to ask ourselves, "What is normal for a twenty-six-year-old stallion?" We didn't know.'

Nevertheless, going by the results, they injected corticosteroids, more powerful antiinflammatories, directly into Slew's articular facets, between his vertebrae. For a while, it looked as if the combination of treatments was going to work – the symptoms let up, and when breeding season started Slew was nimble enough to get six of his first eight mares in foal.

But whenever the medications started to wear off, Slew relapsed into frightening spastic episodes, and though his owners and vets still didn't know what they were dealing with, it was becoming clear that stopgap treatment wasn't going to work. Slew withdrew from stallion service and the treatment went into high gear. 'Between a bone scan and a myelogram, we had a lot of help on this case,' Morehead said. 'I was charged with trying to take care of him, but I had free rein. I could go get whoever I wanted to help in the process. So we actively recruited some of the brighter minds involved with this stuff.'

One of these brighter minds was Barrie Grant. Mickey and Karen Taylor knew about his wobbler surgery; a few weeks after clinching the Triple Crown, Slew galloped at Seattle's Longacres Racetrack, in a benefit for the veterinary research program at Washington State University. They called him up and explained the situation, saying that the time had come to 'kill or cure, because Slew wasn't getting any better and he couldn't escape it'.

Grant brought his team from San Luis Rey Equine Hospital, in California: his fellow surgeons Sandra Valdez and Richard Pankowski and the radiologist Norm Rantanen. The surgical technician, Jan Sargent-Beach, made sure that all the equipment was ready, present, and sharp. (The Taylors had warned Grant: 'Bring your best team and don't screw up.') The anesthesiologist John Hubbell drove down from Ohio State. The fertility specialist Terry Blanchard came up from Texas A&M. Bill Bernard, the head of internal medicine at Rood & Riddle, the veterinary hospital in Lexington where the surgery would be performed, planned to scrub in, in case anything went wrong. All concerned could safely tell themselves that Seattle Slew was getting the best care in the world.

The best care, however, can be hard to watch. On April 2, Slew was put under anesthesia and placed in a padded gurney that kept him on his back – 'dorsal recumbency' is the surgical term, a delicate and poetic phrase to use for a horse turned upside down. On its back under anesthesia, a horse is nearly unrecognizable. The magnificent muscular tension disappears and the legs collapse in such an awkward jumble that they look broken. The vets arrange them quickly, as though leaning broomsticks against a closet wall. The neck falls backward, and the surgeons in their cotton gowns walk up and set it in a brace with an impudently casual confidence. The horse appears to be frozen in a spasm of anguish, eerily immobile, like one of the dogs of Pompeii, upended and petrified in the death struggle.

Neurological surgery on a horse requires an unusual mixture of skills: the nitpicky dexterity of a bomb defuser and a carpenter's ease with power tools. Rantanen, the radiologist, one of maybe five people on earth who could look at a murky X ray (a horse's spine is buried under a three-inch-thick slab of muscle) and have the confidence to say, 'Cut here', advised Grant on the initial placement of the scalpel. Then Grant cut a ten-inch slit to expose a network of arteries and windpipe. He inserted three eight-inch marker pins into Slew's neck, to be sure of the location of the arthritic sixth cervical vertebra. His assistants took the Deaver retractors and retracted the trachea and carotid out of his way; then Grant used a scalpel blade to cut the muscles and fascia overlying the spine and the sixth cervical vertebra. He picked up his drill and made a test hole in the spine, double-checked with Rantanen on the X ray, then drilled the final hole, about as wide as a fifty-cent piece.

Four months before, just about the time when Slew's wobbles began, Bagby came up with another refinement to the Bagby basket. He decided to cut threads on the outside of the cylinder, so the basket could be screwed in. Up to then, they'd been hammering the things into the bone with a stainless-steel mallet – dangerously rough work for spinal surgery. In fact, the pounding had led to spinal fractures and death in 20 per cent of the horses. But since January, when he'd added threads, the fractures had been eliminated. This slight mechanical improvement seems obvious only in retrospect; it took twenty-three years to come up with it.

Once the Bagby basket was screwed in place, Grant and his team began packing the hollow of the stainless-steel cylinder with the live cells of the bone marrow he'd just extracted from the spine. Since the basket (the improved version, with threads, is now called the Seattle Slew basket) has thirty-six holes, the marrow can grow through, fuse with the surrounding bone, and increase the blood supply for healing. When the packing was done, they sewed up the incision; seventy-five minutes after the surgery started, John Hubbell, the anesthesiologist, began to bring Slew back to consciousness. He turned out the lights, since a horse in a dark room was less likely to shy at something and try to get up. Hubbell told everyone that he wanted absolute quiet for at least an hour, although his definition of 'absolute quiet' allowed for Johnny Cash playing softly on a tape.

After seventy-five minutes, Slew finally rolled over onto his chest. Hubbell came up and pulled out the left front leg, Grant pulled out the right one, and the patient stood up without any fuss – another first for Slew, accomplished as usual with little outward indication of what the effort had cost him. As Slew was getting back on his feet, Grant looked at Tom Wade, who'd been there watching from the start, and he saw the tears. 'It was so sweet,' Grant said. 'The horse is straight and you got the groom crying.'

Ten months later, two days before Valentine's Day, the traditional start of breeding season, Tom Wade arrived for work clean shaven. Without the scratchy gray goatee he sported over the winter, he looked younger – fresh-faced and a little impish, like Cupid, only two hundred pounds and in workboots. When people asked, he told them he'd shaved it off for Valentine's, but nobody seemed inclined to believe him. It was eight-thirty AM, February 12, and Dreams of Success, a four-year-old maiden mare who'd just vanned over from nearby Denali Stud, was waiting in the receiving barn. She was being prepped and teased for Seattle Slew – his first 'live cover' in almost a year. If you were in the breeding business, it was the sort of event you might want to look your best for.

Under normal circumstances in Kentucky, a thoroughbred sex act is a team effort, with an average of five active participants, not counting the two horses. But these were not normal circumstances, and the spacious eight-sided breeding shed at Three Chimneys was swarming with powerful folks holding coffee cups, wandering in and out and making small talk on the lawn, waiting for Seattle Slew to, as James Brown once said in a nearly identical situation, 'get up, get on up'.

Mickey and Karen Taylor were on hand, of course. Dr Jim Morehead. Robert Clay, the founder and owner of Three Chimneys. Dan Rosenberg, its president. Barry Weisbord, the co-owner of Dreams of Success. Every last employee in the stallion barn. The Three Chimneys exercise rider. The pedigree consultant. The marketing director. They waited for Slew with a nearly scriptural sense of uncertainty and awe.

But, so far, Slew just wasn't in the mood. It wasn't because he was experiencing any embarrassing incapacity – far from it. Tom Wade had attended all four test breedings arranged by the 'equine reproduction consultant' (the process requires a real mare, but an artificial vagina is artfully substituted at the last possible moment) and, according to Wade: 'First day he goes in there and he's an orangutan.'

No, this felt like something different, closer to what negotiators would call a stunt, and a simple one: Slew wanted to see how long he could keep everyone waiting. It's a favorite ruse of presidential envoys, divorce lawyers, heavyweight champions, and the opposite sex (both of them), but it's a prerogative available only to the party in power, which is why it's a delight to employ and a humiliation to endure.

For a while, everyone tried to ignore the humiliation, focusing instead on Dreams of Success. Morehead gave her a shot of demosedan, a tranquilizer, to 'take a little off her'; Earl, the teaser, was brought into the breeding shed to see how she reacted when he tried a jump. Earl, a hapless and willing draft horse, entered with his heavy leather apron on. He looked like comic relief: the chuck-wagon cook at the shootout. Earl lumbered over to the maiden mare, and when he reared up, she tried to bolt, but he fared a little better on the second jump. He got up and straddled the mare long enough to get her used to the idea – thus earning himself the right to be hauled off and shut back in his stall.

Humiliation isn't the only thing horses seem to have in common with humans. Horses are herd animals, and so are we. Both species survive in groups, keenly attuned to the gestures of dominance and submission in play around us. We both bluff, exaggerate, ignore; maintain alliances, betray loyalties, reward courage, seek affection; we annoy one another out of boredom; we mock our betters; we respond to flattery; we punish and humiliate those we can, and with those we can't we cultivate appearances. We try to get along. We know the real thing when we see it.

Horses communicate all this with a vocabulary of deceptively simple gestures: pawing at the ground, pinning the ears, clicking the teeth, ducking the head, twitching a leg, whipping a tail. Many of these gestures are early warnings of more violent behavior, such as kicking, biting, or charging, but horses rarely need to resort to actual violence, preferring to settle things pretty much as we do, with a quick exchange of threats sincere enough to test the will to violence but symbolic enough to keep the peace and maintain the social contract.

The literature on the social intelligence of horses comes mostly from studying herds of feral horses – Chincoteague ponies on Assateague Island off the coast of Virginia and Maryland; Pryor mountain horses in Lovell, Wyoming; Kiger mustangs in Powell Butte, Oregon; Shetland ponies at the University of Pennsylvania's New Bolton Center. All descend from horses who escaped into the wild or were released into an established feral herd. It's assumed that in these scattered sanctuaries the free-running horses return to their natural arrangement: a powerful stallion with his harem of mares and their young, with bachelor bands of wannabe colts skirting the herd.

But if Slew's behavior is any indication, there's no shortage of complicated social interactions going on at horse farms. And some days, with all the folks hanging around the multimillion-dollar pastureland, waiting on the sexual whims of a recognized sire, it can be hard to tell precisely who domesticated whom.

Nobody could get hold of Slew. He wouldn't let anybody near enough to sweet-talk him. One by one, Mickey, Tom, and Karen straggled out of Slew's private barn in varying shades of frustration.

'We've been through an apple and a carrot and we still haven't got him,' Mickey said. 'We wait ten months for this and then we can't catch him.'

A few minutes later, Karen came over to Mickey. She said, 'He knew as soon as I turned the radio up that something was going on. He's just walking around now.'

So, what was Slew listening to?

'Reiki music,' Karen said, referring to the sort of waterfall-and-harp arrangements you normally find playing in the waiting rooms of aromatherapists. 'He started with cowboy Western. We put on reiki music to chill him out sometimes. Or Pavarotti. What he really likes is Andre Bocelli.'

Another mare had arrived in the meantime, and Sandy Hatfield decided there was only so long she could make the filly wait. She called across the quad for Dynaformer, a giant of a horse, seventeen hands high, who had a reputation around the farm for being two things: dumb and overendowed. He pranced down the path to the breeding shed half erect, springing along like a satyr in a semi-crouch, ready to plant and mount as soon as he spotted an available target. Horses often seem soulful and mysteriously engaged with matters we have no inkling of; Dynaformer ('Big D') did not. If his inner life had subtitles, the dialogue we'd have been reading just then ('Hoo-boy! Babe alert!') wouldn't have sounded all that different from his actual repertoire of grunts.

Big D's endowment requires extra care in the breeding shed. A larger stallion can tear or bruise the cervix of a small or maiden mare, so somebody on the team has to stand by with a 'breeding roll' – a sort of bolster pillow or padded rolling pin about five to eight inches in diameter designed to cushion the blows and lessen the erectile yardage. (Three Chimneys has three sizes of breeding rolls to choose from. Dynaformer is the only one to get the extra-large.) The designated pillow man has to be pretty deft, a real swordsman in his own right, to be able to poke the breeding roll between the mare's rump and the stallion's tummy, just above the penis, and he has to time his thrust to coincide with that brief instant just after Big D manages to gain his first inch of access but well before he succeeds in burying himself to the hilt.

To maintain hygiene, the breeding roll is often covered with one of the plastic gloves that the vet wears to perform palpations, so you can tell that the pillow man has succeeded only when you see a ghostly inflated hand waving at you out of the action zone.

Dynaformer was quick – it was so early in the season that even the most reluctant breeders were snappy at their work. Afterward, quiet as a petting-zoo pony, he was led out of the breeding shed, back across the quad, past the bronze statue of Seattle Slew on the pedestal in the center of the stallion complex.

Tom Wade had come over to help with the mating. As he watched the suddenly pliant Dynaformer being led back to his stall after his first maiden mare of the season, Wade yelled, 'Next!' Then, as if he'd just figured out that he was the only one who could carry out the order, he walked back to Slew's barn alone.

So what do people on one of the world's top breeding farms do when their legendary stallion just won't show? They wait. They check sperm samples under the microscope. They tell tall tales. Mickey Taylor remembered that when Will Farish brought his filly Weekend Surprise over to Spendthrift, Slew kept them waiting that morning, too. And that was the mating that made A. P. Indy, he said, as if to imply that all Seattle Slew needed to deliver a champion horse and Belmont Stakes and Breeders' Cup Classic winner like A. P. Indy was a little windup.

Dan Rosenberg, noticing how everyone was milling around the barn like groupies waiting backstage for a rock star, remembered a Jefferson Airplane concert he'd attended. The band didn't even show up, let alone walk onstage, until everyone had been made to wait for an hour.

'Maybe he didn't get the news about the mare,' Mickey said to Rosenberg, who sent shareholders and syndicate members frequent informative updates on Slew's condition. 'Did you have him on the e-mail list?'

Mickey didn't seem to think that computer literacy was incon-
ceivable. After all, Slew had been first at everything else. If anything,
Mickey's mood seemed to brighten as the wait grew longer, as if the
unusual delay had helped refresh his memory of all the other days
when Slew managed to pull off something unusual. He talked about
the first time the Three Chimneys exercise rider tried to gallop him.
That was another morning when nobody could get hold of Slew.
By the time the rider got up in the saddle, 'Slew'd scared the living
loving shit out of him.' Mickey chuckled.

Taylor had a fine and firsthand appreciation of fear. Growing up
in Washington's Ellensburg Valley, he and his high-school buddies
used to corral wild mustangs in Dead Man's Chute, then sell the
beasts to riders on the rodeo circuit. As he followed Wade's path
back to Slew's barn, you could see him settling into his adrenaline
rush with a nostalgic smirk.

As the woolgathering session came to a close, Dreams of
Success was led from the loading dock back to the breeding
shed. At first, her forced return seemed like nothing more than a
hopeful, half-magical gesture, made the way someone at a bus
stop might light a cigarette to make the bus finally appear. But
then, as one of the handlers bent down to put the padded boots
onto the hooves of her hind (and prime kicking) legs, a nearby
stallion yelled, and the mare shook off the loose boots and looked
back over her shoulder.

'He's coming,' somebody said.

Finally Seattle Slew emerged from his stable, with Tom Wade
holding the lead shank beside him, and the Taylors, Mickey and
Karen (the latter observing it all through her video camera),
following dutifully behind: a quartet of creatures all rendered
youthful for the moment by the morning's historic mission. Slew
looked spring-loaded, prancing and threatening at once, taking his
time as he paced over the path toward the eastern entrance to the

breeding shed, once again fully aware, it seemed, of his power and his easy command.

In the breeding shed, the handlers were ready, even if the mare was not. One of them held her left front leg off the ground with a leather strap; another distracted her as much as he could with a twitch. (A twitch is a big long stick with a loop of rope at the end that's applied to the filly's upper lip and then twisted to distract her – an advance in veterinary medicine that dates to about the Middle Ages.) Despite this diversionary pain, the four-year-old mare (a grandchild, like Storm Cat, of the great Canadian sire Northern Dancer) rolled her eyes back to follow Seattle Slew's progress toward her, across the barn's two-foot bed of wood chips, laid down fresh for the season – soft footing for the rearing stallions, to preserve their bones.

Slew had entered the room just as ready to perform as Dynaformer, eleven years his junior. But you could see the differences in approach that morning. Dynaformer had a rude and unceremonious style – two hops and on, just the sort of dangerous directness that would have won him few repeat engagements had his life been different, had he been obliged to charm his partners instead of having them tied down for him. Slew, however, despite the long time away and his very evident arousal, had not forgotten his manners: he nuzzled the mare, moving from the shoulder where she was restrained, down her flank, bringing his lips, in the sort of gesture he'd use to test the tenderness of a patch of grass, hesitantly down her flank, moving closer and closer toward the business that he had nearly given up for good ten months before.

She held still for his kindness.

Even the snappiest operations, which can wash, tease, breed, and lead away a stallion in less time than it takes to play a Top Forty tune, make time for this sort of intimacy – which is somehow harder and more embarrassing to witness than anything that follows. The stallion handler loosens his hold on the lead shank and, usually, observes a respectful silence as the stallion runs through his limited foreplay options – kiss, nudge, nibble, sniff. The mare raises her tail. Because, by this point, the arousal is usually mutual, the anatomy that she bares for his perusal pulses unmistakably. Horse breeders call it winking, which is an accurate description of the gesture: 'clapping' would be a good word if you wanted to capture the scale.

But it didn't matter what you called it. Slew had already decided it was time to come hither, anyway. He stepped back to choose his angle, and the Three Chimneys team, many of whom had been keeping tabs on the incremental increase in his excitement the way day traders track the upticks of a favorite stock, scurried to their places. He reared up and brought himself down on the maiden mare.

Unfortunately, he ended up about a yard off and sideways, either as a result of eagerness or because he was out of practice. Tom Wade yanked him down, and Slew stood there flatfooted for a while, in a fair imitation of his own bronze statue.

Actually, the first jump might have been strategy, a little cautious testing of his own, the sort of see-for-himself behavior he might dust off when he spots a potentially dangerous maiden mare. Most of the stories about Slew's intelligence strongly suggest the presence of a cautious, even finicky streak. Not to make a joke about it, but Slew can be something of a naysayer, which can make him come off as gruff or high-handed. He looks down at you – you don't catch *his* eye so much as *he* takes *you* in. You see only one eye at a time, of course – he's a horse – but the eye is famous. It's dark amber and skeptical, filled with rough, country patience, and for as long as he holds your gaze you know two things: you know he's thinking, and you know you don't know what. The two things almost cancel each other out, so you can walk away from the encounter, as you often do in the country, with a lasting impression of the inexpressible.

Slew quickly collected himself and reared again, and this time he found the mark. There was nothing arthritic about him. He grabbed hold of her neck with his teeth and, in about seven powerful demonstrations of fully functional spinal flexibility, he made it official. Three Chimneys' top stud was back.

He returned to earth about thirty seconds later and took a last wistful look as they led away his day's work. As Tom Wade walked him back to his stall, Dan Rosenberg, turned to me and said cheerfully, 'There's one less maiden mare in the bluegrass.'

SEVEN

Young Stud Enters the
Family Business

I F Y O U ' R E A F I R S T - T I M E Kentucky stud, chances are you'll lose your virginity in January, with an older female, just for practice. The weather will be cold, but you won't care. You will get so hot that the steam coming off your body in the unheated barn will nearly make you disappear from sight. As for your performance, which will be recorded on videotape, you will be inept and excitable, which will make everybody around you jumpy, since you have a good chance of falling off in the middle of the proceedings or, when they are over, of collapsing onto the floor in a faint.

Your partner will be nothing like you: she'll be easy and agreeable and slow to react. She will be in heat. She will be big to the point of immobility and she will have an unmistakably large behind, to give you, according to Wes Lanter, 'a solid platform for learning the ways of the world'. Despite her width, she will be shorter than you; or, if she is not, you will work from the top of a pitcher's mound, so you can reach.

If you're incredibly lucky, like Cat Thief, a five-year-old son of Storm Cat, you'll end up at Overbrook Farm, where no matter how badly you bungle your first day, they'll still know exactly what to do. In fact, on the morning of Cat Thief's on-the-job training, everyone in the barn looks loose and relaxed, the coffee is 'stout' –

that's Kentucky for strong – and the conversation has turned to girls named Jughead. One of the grooms claims that his first girlfriend, from Woodford County, was named Jughead. Wes Lanter says he worked with a guy who called his wife Jughead, or, when he was feeling romantic, Jugs.

Jughead, it turns out, is also the name of Cat Thief's first: a Belgian draft mare of indeterminate age, whose amenable temperament makes her the perfect candidate for this line of work. Her ovaries have been removed, so whenever her services are required, all it takes to get her in heat is an injection of synthetic estrogen. I ask Lanter how Jughead got her name and he says, 'When you see her you'll know why.'

It's true. A few minutes later, Jughead trudges into the padded chute in the receiving barn – 'the stocks' where Kevin Stephens will wash her up and wrap her tail in surgical bandages – and, indeed, her head is huge. Lanter holds out a new halter that he wants Stephens, who prepares the mares for the breeding shed, to put on her. 'It took two cows to make that halter,' he says. As Stephens works on her back end, Jughead stands with unblinking patience, the breath billowing out of her nostrils like steam from the Times Square Cup O' Noodles sign.

Despite the cold, the door to the receiving barn is kept open, and once Jughead is ready to go to the breeding shed, Lanter steps out to watch for Cat Thief's arrival. It's an overcast morning, and across the gray sky an out-of-season V of geese goes honking by. 'We got the most open water between here and . . . somewhere,' Stephens explains. Pioneering, an eight-year-old half-brother to Storm Cat, starts knowingly patrolling the breeding-shed side of his paddock. 'She's not for you,' Stephens tells him, and then, as Cat Thief arrives (with none of the fancy prancing you see on the horses who know what they're in for), Stephens, too, heads to the shed. He says with a workaday irony, 'OK, yippee, cai-yi-yo.'

Like all first-timers, Cat Thief seems clueless about basic technique. Jughead stands on one side of the barn, giving him any number of unequivocal signs. She spreads her legs like a sawhorse and begins winking. Her behaviour is the equine equivalent of coming out of the shower, dropping the towel, and saying, 'Hey, sailor. Welcome ashore.' Cat Thief is the only one around with absolutely no clue about what's going on. Instead of approaching her, he grows intensely interested in the chain in his mouth. He bites it; he tosses his head so the chain makes a funny noise against his teeth; he takes another bite, but at a different angle. His behavior is the equine equivalent of pulling out his Game Boy.

To interrupt this pointless reverie, John Fahey tugs hard on the lead shank and takes Cat Thief over to Jughead's hind end, where, despite a complete failure in the suave department, the novice stallion appears ready to perform almost immediately. After his first brush of direct contact and with little preparation, he rears up and enters Jughead. Lanter says, 'Come on, son.'

But in the middle of everything, the horse seems either to return to his senses or lose them completely, and he stops, drawing himself up, as if to say, 'How did I get here?'

'Quit playing, now,' Lanter says. He then gives him a little push from behind and says, 'Work, bud.' Cat Thief resumes, going at it for a while with what seems like wholehearted resolve, then drops inexplicably back to the ground.

'Aw. He was right there.'

Lanter and Stephens go over the inventory of backup mares. ('What about Ashley?') But since Jughead is here and willing, they decide to make this work. Cat Thief is again led to her back end. Again he rears. Again he loses something – his rhythm? his concentration? his grip? – and falls off. They let him step back and collect himself. He stands alone for a moment, steam rising off his back and rump and shoulders like dry ice swirling around a stadium rocker.

Doc Yocum, the Overbrook vet, who has been standing near the door to the stallion-barn office, mentions the cold, which, if you don't happen to be thermally evolved and currently engaging in a sexual act, is bad enough to make you hunch over and complain.

'Doc, I got another million-dollar idea,' Lanter says, as he prepares to guide Cat Thief, once again, into his starter mare. 'Rubber gloves with jersey linings.'

Once again, Cat Thief sticks around for a few thrusts and falls off. 'Goddammit.'

Deciding that Jughead is too tall for the young horse, they lead the pair over to the pitcher's mound. By this point, both animals are steaming, and on the third go, with Cat Thief up on the hill, the process works just the way it's supposed to. The son of Storm Cat looks like a pro, quick and tidy, with a little flare of the tail at the end.

'There you go!'

But when he falls off, he seems unsteady on his feet, and he shakes his head – in wonder, bafflement, and a score of other obvious emotions that according to the behaviorists he is incapable of. Still, he looks about as surprised as a horse can look. As a rule, horses do not place a premium on new experiences, so Cat Thief seems doubly surprised, by the unfamiliar experience and by the idea that the unfamiliar could prove so overwhelmingly satisfying. Maybe, after he shook his head, Cat Thief never gave the whole event a second thought, but his astounded shiver seems to have thrown everybody in the barn into private and unconfessable reflection. 'Daddy never told me about this,' Stephens says finally, and leads the horse over to be washed.

Being completely unaware – of the technique, of the expectations, of the potential lifelong financial consequences – is normal for a first-timer, and Cat Thief is like most (people and horses) in his level of obliviousness. But because he is the latest in a line of sons of Storm Cat to assume a position in the family business, Cat Thief's brief visit to the breeding shed has set a complicated financial machinery in motion.

Cat Thief comes from a solid financial background. His mother, Train Robbery, won more than $600,000 in her four years at the track. That seems like a lot, but Overbrook had spent $350,000 at the Keeneland sales to buy her, so she had to win quite a few before she could start turning a profit. In some ways, Cat Thief, who brought in nearly $4 million at the track, can be considered the return, ten years later, on that original 1986 investment. 'He danced every dance,' Bob Warren, the Overbrook CPA, told me. That's a standard saying around the racetrack, a polite form of lukewarm praise. What it really means is that Cat Thief didn't win often (only four times in three years), but was a steady earner, running in the money in twenty-one of his thirty mostly top-flight races.

But, as with any commodity, past returns are no indication of future performance. The odds against Cat Thief – the odds against any 'freshman sire' – ever making it to the list of leading sires are daunting. In every incoming class, only one or two (out of approximately fifteen thousand colts born each year) will ever reach the top of their profession. Consider Storm Cat and his peers: only four horses born in 1983, the same year as Storm Cat, have ascended to the list of the top fifty sires (ranked by the racetrack earnings of their offspring), and only Broad Brush, who stands for $100,000 at Gainesway, attracts anything like the sort of big-money, best-family mares that Storm Cat does.

Luckily for Cat Thief, there is a wonderfully illogical optimism to the breeding business, and the stud fees of first-year stallions regularly exceed those of proven sires. Why? Because breeders think they have a real shot at buying right into a great pedigree, and they seem willing to pay premium prices for this chance at greatness. But this burst of fiscal optimism, Cat Thief's grace period, only lasts so long – as soon as a horse begins a career at stud, the clock starts ticking. In the first year at stud, breeders ask, *How did he do at the track?* The second year, *How do his foals look?* The fourth year, *How did his yearlings sell?* By the fifth year – when the breeders can open the *Racing Form* to see whether the babies can actually run – the fate of a stallion is essentially sealed. By that time, what a horse did at the track barely matters, and his stud fee begins to reflect the true market value of his offspring, at the track and in the sales ring.

In other words, if Cat Thief's kids aren't winning big races by 2004, he'll probably end up like Mountain Cat and Tabasco Cat, other sons of Storm Cat who now ply their trade for the Türkiye Jokey Kulübü, in Izmit, Turkey, and Shizunai Stallion Station, in Hokkaido, Japan, respectively.

But during his first few seasons, before Cat Thief ever establishes his own value as a sire, breeders are willing to take a chance on him because he comes from an illustrious lineage, with three hundred years of nearly uninterrupted victories and impeccable breeding. It's easy to study his sireline and get the idea that Cat Thief could be the next great stud. For example, on the following quick tour through his ancestry, notice how often the sireline detours, and a leading sire is sired by the *son* of a leading sire.

Cat Thief's sireline begins in 1704, when the Darley Arabian was smuggled out of Turkey by Thomas Darley, in violation of a two-century-old Ottoman prohibition against the export of purebred Arabians. The Darley Arabian begat Bartlett's (Bleeding) Childers, who begat Squirt, who begat Marske, who begat the champion Eclipse, who was born in Windsor Great Park, the Duke of Cumberland's estate, on April 1, 1764, a day when the moon covered the sun.

Eclipse, unbeaten as a racehorse and, according to eyewitnesses, unsurpassed as a sire, begat Pot-8-O's, who got his name, according to legend, when a barely literate stablehand, told to write 'Potatoes' on the door of the stall, put down 'POTOOOOOOOO', the latter portion of which was later shortened to '8-O's'. Pot-8-O's begat Waxy, who won the Epsom Derby for the 3rd Duke of Grafton, one of the dumber prime ministers of England, who built twelve cushy miles of a projected eighteen-mile grass avenue from his estate, Euston Hall, to the races at Newmarket before realizing that his intended route would cross somebody else's property. Waxy begat Whalebone, who was born in 1807, the same year that Thomas Jefferson shut down the American whaling industry to make the Old World understand a point he was making about maritime trade.

Whalebone begat Sir Hercules, who stood at Summerhill, Lord Langford's estate in Ireland. Sir Hercules begat Birdcatcher (sometimes called the Irish Birdcatcher), who stood at Lord Rossmore's Brownstown Stud, also in Ireland, where he begat The Baron, a 'rough, snappish customer', who was bred to Pocahontas, and begat Stockwell, who raced for the Marquis of Exeter and stood at Hooton Hall. All of the 'Irish' horses listed above were owned by English lords and miscellaneous English gentry.

Stockwell begat Doncaster, who despite being described as 'big, backward, and unfurnished' and 'too gross' to get into racing condition, went on to win the Epsom Derby, at odds of forty-five to one. Doncaster begat Bend Or, which may be the one stupid pun in the entire genealogy. Bend Or was born in 1877, and owned by Hugh Lupus Grosvenor, 1st Duke of Westminster, as was Tadcaster, another Doncaster colt born in 1877. A controversy arose when a groom who was about to be fired from the family's Eaton Stud claimed that the two nearly identical colts, with matching black spots on their rumps, had been exchanged after exercise. The resulting confusion between the two persisted until Bend Or began siring fillies who looked exactly like his mother, Rouge Rose, a roomy mare who also handed down to her granddaughters her one great vice: cribbing, an overwhelming desire to grab fences with the teeth and take great gulps of air.

Apart from these obsessive-compulsive fillies, Bend Or begat Bona Vista, who was owned by Hannah de Rothschild, the wife of Archibald Philip Primrose, the 5th Earl of Rosebery. Primrose was a subtle foreign secretary under Gladstone and was briefly prime minister, from March 1894, to the spring of 1895, a period that saw the ouster of the Liberal Party, as well as Bona Vista's first season at stud, during which he begat Cyllene. Cyllene remained in England long enough to beget Polymelus, who was owned by Solly Joel, the largest individual stockholder in the De Beers mining conglomerate, and the sole witness to the mysterious death at sea of his uncle, Barney Barnato, from whom he inherited the vast tracts of South African land that later became Johannesburg.

Polymelus begat Phalaris out of a mare belonging to Edward George Villiers Stanley, the 17th Earl of Derby, for whose family the race is named. The Earl served as secretary of war during the First World War, although his political ambitions were handicapped by bouts of dithering in a crisis: at one point, when the British army was to be placed under French command, the Earl submitted his resignation and withdrew it again three times in twenty-four hours, according to the then prime minister, Lloyd George. In matters of breeding, however, Lord Derby was decisive and authoritative, and it was his belief that a well-researched mating should be practiced repeatedly. Which is why Phalaris was bred to Scapa Flow ten times in twelve years, begetting first Pharos, then Fairway, Fara, Fair Isle, Pharillon, etc.

Pharos was a sprinter who faded in the longer important races, unlike his brother Fairway, who won the St Leger Stakes, the oldest and longest of Britain's three classic races. When he graduated to stud duties, Fairway went straight to the top of the sire lists as soon as his children hit the track. The Italian breeder Federico Tesio wanted to send his finely built champion filly Nogara to the rangy Fairway, but Derby's stud manager, a Captain Paine, turned down the application, either because Fairway was completely booked or because Paine found Tesio to be 'a contemptible little foreigner'. Tesio was forced to settle for the runty and second-rate speed horse Pharos, whom Derby had already packed off to Haras d'Ouilly, France.

So Pharos, not Fairway, begat Nearco, whom Tesio considered the finest achievement of his career. To horse traders on a tight budget, Tesio is an inspiring figure. Few breeders could be called his equal, and on that short list, which would include the Earl of Derby and the Aga Khan, Tesio was by far the poorest, with a knack for picking up cheap mares from good families, breeding them to the best stallions he could afford, and turning out crop after crop of classic winners.

He was a solitary man, orphaned as a boy, and, like so many in the breeding business, childless. As a young cavalry officer, he rode with the gauchos across the Argentine pampas, and in his maturity he preserved something of the gaucho's impatience for town-and-country ways. At the races, he watched his horses from the rail, stoop-shouldered and alone, and at the Newmarket auctions he left other breeders to their own society. When he came to look over stallions at the British stud farms, he was capable of watching a horse for minutes on end, then leaving without a word. At Villa Dormello, his stud farm on the banks of Lago Maggiore, he and his wife, Lydia, were hardly self-sufficient — he ran a racing stable in partnership with the Marchese Mario Incisa della Rocchetta — but the couple lived with studied simplicity. He built Art Deco furniture, she kept the books.

He gave his horses names like Donatello, Botticelli, Bellini, Van Dyck, and he named Nearco after a secondary character in a

Donizetti opera who refuses to betray Christians to Roman author-
ities. This assessment of character held: on the racecourse, Nearco
was unyielding, and so fast that it cast doubts on his stamina. Tesio
kept expecting the colt to fail at greater distances, but Nearco kept
winning. In 1938, at Longchamp for the Grand Prix de Paris, in his
final test against the best company, he beat a field of twenty that
included the undefeated winner of the English Derby. It was an
emphatic climax to Nearco's unbeaten racing career, but Tesio's
pleasure in it was tragically brief. As the Italian horse strode into the
winner's circle under police escort, the Parisian crowd jeered and
the jockey, Pietro Gubellini, responded with a Fascist salute. The
only evidence that this mortified Tesio is this: within days, in
violation of Mussolini's orders and despite efforts by the Italian
embassy to block the export of a national treasure, Tesio sold the
horse to an English bookie, Martin Benson. Nearco never again
stepped on Italian soil.

Was Tesio antifascist? He was high-handed, reclusive, intuitive,
and obsessed. On his favorite topic, he was by turns charming and
purposely obscure, and he seemed to regard any interruption in his
work as almost a moral evil. Here is Tesio on war: 'In February
1945, the area of my farm at Dormello on Lake Maggiore was
bombed several times. The bridge at Sesto Calende, the munitions
factory at Taino, and the aircraft factory were hit. The windows of
the villa and those of the stables were shattered. But the horses never
showed any particular signs of fear, except on one occasion when
the very pasture in which they were grazing was dive-bombed. And
what is more, the bombing caused no abortions among the mares in
foal, as we had reason to fear.'

At Benson's Beech House Stud, Nearco begat Nearctic after a
typically convoluted transatlantic horse-trading deal. The buyer, the
Canadian brewing magnate E. P. Taylor, believed in the Earl of
Derby's multiple-matings theory, so when he found a broodmare in

foal to Nearco, he insisted that she be bred to the Italian champion again as a condition of the sale. Taylor wound up with three horses: the broodmare, Lady Angela; Empire Day, the forgettable horse she was pregnant with at the time of the deal; and Nearctic, the result of the return breeding Taylor'd insisted upon.

Nearctic was the Canadian two-year-old champion in 1956, but he came up lame the following winter and missed the 1957 Kentucky Derby. He recovered in time to win the Michigan Mile, in July, the richest race ever won by a Canadian horse, and the following month Taylor took the $40,000 purse to the Saratoga sales and spent it on a yearling filly he called Natalma. But Taylor ran into the same heartbreak with her: after an exceptionally fast workout at Churchill Downs, the week before the Kentucky Oaks (the fillies' version of the Derby), Natalma came up lame, and her racing career was over. Since there was still a month left in the breeding season, Taylor hurried the maiden mare to the shed. She went to Taylor's newest (and most fertile) stallion.

Which is how, on one visit, Nearctic begat Northern Dancer, a bay colt with a big blaze and a pencil-thin half circle over his right eye, like a raised eyebrow. It gave the tiny horse a curious, half-questioning look, freezing his expression in a sort of friendly Canadian 'Eh?' But the impression of amiability was misleading; Northern Dancer had a nasty temper and, once he hit the track, an explosive move. As a two-year-old in training, on his first day working out of a starting gate, the 'midget' that nobody wanted to buy nearly set a track record, and on May 2, 1964, at the ninetieth running of the Kentucky Derby, he did. Since that day, only three horses have run the route faster: Secretariat and Sham, in the 1974 Derby, and Monarchos, in 2001.

Northern Dancer won the Preakness two weeks later, but fell one race short of the Triple Crown, when he lost the last and longest race, the Belmont. Because of that loss, as he began his stud career many of the top breeders wrote him off as the perfect example of a small, fast horse whose offspring wouldn't 'get the ground'. That changed for good in 1970, when the Irish trainer Vincent O'Brien took Nijinsky, a colt out of Northern Dancer's second crop, and won the English Triple Crown – the Two Thousand Guineas, the Epsom Derby, and the St Leger Stakes. 'You could ride him with a silver thread,' said Nijinsky's jockey Liam Ward. 'Pull him out and say "Go" and that was it.'

Nijinsky's success attracted European buyers to the Kentucky auctions, who drove up the sale prices of Northern Dancers to unprecedented levels. In the eighties, the top eleven colts sold at Keeneland's July sale went for sums ranging from $4.25 million to $13.1 million; seven of them were Northern Dancers and three were Nijinskys. These high-priced horses could run, too: both Coolmore and the sheikhs got multiple European champions out of Northern Dancer. The following is fairly typical of what was happening at the highest level of racing at the time: In 1980, Sheikh Mohammed bought a Northern Dancer colt for $3.3 million and gave it to his brother Sheikh Maktoum Al Maktoum, naming the horse Shareef Dancer, after descendants of the Prophet Mohammed who ruled Mecca. Shareef Dancer won the Irish Derby, the first classic win for the brothers from Dubai. The horse he beat was a Nijinsky colt, Caerleon, owned by Coolmore. Later, in the summer, Coolmore and Sheikh Mohammed dueled again, at Keeneland, in a bidding war over a Northern Dancer colt. Again the Sheikh won, paying $10.2 million for a horse he called Snaafi Dancer, who never raced and turned out to be sterile.

In 1979, Coolmore paid a million dollars for Storm Bird, a Northern Dancer colt out of E. P. Taylor's mare South Ocean. As a two-year-old, Storm Bird won the Dewhurst stakes, at Newmarket, and the Anglesey stakes, the Aga Kahn, and the National Stakes, at the Curragh, all in dominating fashion, and he was named Europe's champion two-year-old. Dominant wins at two are considered the sign of a promising stallion (many breeders consider precocious muscular development as evidence of testosterone to spare), and there were great hopes for the brilliant juvenile. But in the winter, a groom who'd been fired from Ballydoyle, Vincent O'Brien's training center in Tipperary, sneaked back onto the grounds at night and hacked off Storm Bird's mane and tail. The horse grew depressed, lost interest in his gallops, and raced only once more, finishing without passion in the middle of the pack.

Coolmore still managed to sell him, on the strength of his two-year-old year, to an American breeding farm for $28 million; in his first breeding season at Ashford Stud, in Versailles, Kentucky, Storm Bird begat Storm Cat, out of a Secretariat mare, Terlingua. Terlingua had been trained by the former quarter-horse trainer D. Wayne Lukas; she was Lukas's first great success in the Thoroughbred ranks. After her racing career, W. T. Young bought her for Overbrook Farm, sending her first to the son of Northern Dancer, Lyphard, and the following year to Storm Bird, who begat Storm Cat.

By his own admission, Young paid high prices to get the best available mares; he simply had to if he wanted to get into the business, as he did in 1980, at the age of sixty-two, after turning over to his son the management of W. T. Young, Inc. Another thing he had to do was clear about fourteen jalopies out of the creek bed on the property he'd bought, the old Overbrook dairy farm on the southeastern edge of Lexington. Young is one of the last of the friendly, modest men of great accomplishment whom, according to old movies, this country used to be full of, and, in true Jimmy Stewart fashion, he can seem genuinely surprised by his good fortune. 'It is hard for me to realize Storm Cat is recognized as the top stallion today,' he wrote in one of his prompt, polite letters responding to my questions. 'Credit has to go somewhere besides me even though we bred him.'

The connection between wealth and horses goes back to the beginnings of civilization. The connection between the Thoroughbred and the upper classes is far more recent, and in typical English fashion, it almost ended in a bloodbath before it ever began. During England's Civil War, Oliver Cromwell and the antiroyalist forces made a point of destroying the great stud farms like the Tutbury stud of Charles I and the Earl of Newcastle's Welbeck Abbey stud, not because their horses were tactically essential in war, but because even then they were sport horses. Cromwell's Council of State banned horseracing, and his forces killed, scattered, and sold the royalist horses indiscriminately.

In 1660, two years after the death of Cromwell, Charles II succeeded to the throne. As the Restoration dawned, one of the first things the Merry Monarch thought to restore was horseracing. Charles delighted in it; he is the king referred to in the phrase 'the sport of kings'. He set up royal stables and a country palace at Newmarket and established the King's Plate races, a series of three four-mile heats. The royal court and various mistresses (the Duchess of Portsmouth, the Duchess of Cleveland, the Duchess of Mazarin) attended; one mistress, Nell Gwynne, kept a house there. Like his current namesake, Charles appeared freely with his mistress in public. The king's sexual appetites were honored in the nickname 'Old Rowley', which he shared with his favorite stallion.

The length of the King's Plate races required the importation of stallions who could pass on the stamina that British horses lacked. 'Oriental' stallions, either purebreds like the Darley Arabian or, more often, special export hybrids of Arabian and Turkoman breeds, were shipped back to England from trading centers like Turkey, Morocco, and the Barbary Coast, often as the gift of allies who knew of the English preoccupation with racing. These stallions, who appear in the records as the 'Old Morocco Barb', 'Byerly Turk', 'Bloody Shouldered Arabian', and so on, were mated to speedy local mares: English hackneys, Scottish Galloways, and Irish Hobby horses.

There followed a period of about a hundred years or so when an incredibly small and inbred population raced for the pleasure of ditto, often to the accompaniment of cockfights, the winners to receive not only the purses staked by subscribers (His Grace the Duke of Bolton, twenty guineas; Right Hon. the Lord William Manners, twenty guineas; Sir William Morgan, Knight of the Bath, twenty guineas, etc.) but other awards as well, including frequently a plate of some value and many hogsheads of claret. Toward the end of this period, around 1752, the Jockey Club, the body that to this day oversees the sport and maintains the breed, was established, whimsically and obscurely, out of the Star and Garter, in Pall Mall, London, the same tavern where the rules of cricket were refined in 1755, and where, ten years after *that*, Lord Byron, grand-uncle of the poet, ran a sword through his cousin William Chatworth, in a dueling room, after an argument over the proper way to hang game.

The nobles and sporting gentlemen of the Jockey Club quickly extended their influence, banishing cheaters, inaugurating races, and building themselves a proper headquarters, in Newmarket, known as the Coffee Room. They also approved the efforts of Mr James Weatherby to compile a 'General Stud-book, containing with very few exceptions the pedigree of every horse, mare, etc., of note that has appeared on the Turf for the last fifty years, and many of an earlier date, arranged in a peculiar manner'.

It is hard to know what prompted this effort. Presumably, everyone hoped that Weatherby's book would help eliminate fraudulent entries of racehorses, a new but growing anxiety in horseracing. The original guidelines for the sport, Charles II's

Articles of Racing, were explicitly democratic. They permitted entry for any horse, mare, stallion, or gelding: the only principle of selection was the difficulty of the King's Plate race itself. But under George III, horseracing had exploded – it was just the sort of lighthearted distraction a king requires when he is losing both his colonies and his sanity. And the new races tended to be short, like the two-mile St Leger and the mile-and-a-half Epsom Derby, requiring horses with less stamina and more speed. Breeders stopped importing expensive Turks, Barbs, and Arabs and relied instead on older English lines, sometimes of unverified descent. Unraced mares, out of neglected sprinting lines, were sent to the breeding shed, in hopes of producing the new speed horse.

The anxiety about the pedigrees of bloodstock probably accompanied other, profounder anxieties. For decades, the fitness and good breeding of horses had been guaranteed as much by the title, lineage, and social standing of the owners as by any inherent hereditary qualifications of their stock. But times were changing, and all sorts of people were now buying in. When the Duke of Cumberland, a founding member of the Jockey Club, died in 1765, his yearling Eclipse was sold in a dispersal sale to a Mr William Wildman. The duke did not live to see the vindication of his breeding theories (more speed, less pedigree); instead the great Eclipse, by Marske, out of Spiletta, rode under the colors of a Smithfield grazier and meat merchant.

Of course, it could also be argued that Jockey Club members were scarcely the anxious type, and that when it came right down to it they had no objections to selling a horse to satisfy the odd gambling debt. In any event, they were certainly not the sort to spend all evening quibbling about some laudable but eccentric little project – comprehensive studbook, containing pedigrees, and so on – and the matter seems to have passed with no objection. *Smashing! Here, here! To Weatherby, then!*

Weatherby was well equipped for the task. For many years, he'd been the editor of the annual racing calendar, a position that became hereditary with him and carried the title Keeper of the Match Book at Newmarket. The position gave him access to race results, sales papers, and the breeders themselves. The private studbooks he consulted to make his compilation were more or less casual notations whose accuracy varied from farm to farm. Some stud farms, like the Earl of Newcastle's Welbeck Abbey, or the Dinsdale estate that Mr Cuthbert Routh acquired from Cromwell's stud master, kept meticulous records; others relied on the memory of their 'yeomen of the race', as stallion managers were then called.

Weatherby published his first *General Stud Book* in 1791. It was an impressive and novel accomplishment, but by today's standards it was laughably small: the first edition contains the pedigrees of only 387 mares, each of whom could be traced back to one of three great race champions, Eclipse, Matchem, or Herod, descended in turn from three imported stallions, the Darley Arabian, the Godolphin Arabian, and the Byerly Turk, respectively. (The Jockey Club currently maintains a database of over 1.8 million Thoroughbred horses, all of whom, they contend, descend from these three.)

The first edition was intended as a descriptive reference for breeders and buyers, and made no pretense of founding a breed or 'closing the stud book' for ever – although (after a few subsequent editions) that was its effect. It began as a catalogue of pedigrees, a sort of instruction manual for breeders to study (and perhaps thereby to reproduce) the matings that led to a champion, but it grew to have a tremendous impact. It became a lasting work of modest genius, the first expression of a national obsession with breeding (of both the noble and barnyard varieties) that led to Darwin. Weatherby set out simply to take inventory and correct false pedigrees, but in the process, he practically invented the idea of the 'breed', that is, a group of creatures whose bloodlines are carefully maintained in separation from others of their species. In a sense, all creatures of pedigree – borzois, Brahman bulls, Nubian goats, angora cats – descend from this first inventory. Even the nobility who owned the Thoroughbreds that he catalogued had no centralized registry to keep track of their own lineages; Weatherby's studbook predates the first edition of *Burke's Peerage* by thirty-five years.

Twenty-one updates of the *General Stud Book* were published over the next century. Overlooked mares were added, questionable dams expunged (it was discovered that Copenhagen, the charger that the Duke of Wellington rode at Waterloo, descended from a mere hunting mare), exports noted, certification procedures detailed, and entertaining fulminations indulged, like this one, from a Colonel Gilbert Ironside, from the 1800 edition:

> It is remarkable, however, that scarcely any fleet coursers sprang from the celebrated Childers, though himself the swiftest horse ever known; on the contrary, his racers have proved eminently defective, declining, like our modern nobility, with an uncommon precipitation of degeneracy.

Harebrained conclusions based on zoological minutiae were as typical of the nineteenth century as weird facial hair. Still, the colonel had a point. Once a king has addressed the court as 'My Lords and Peacocks', as George III did, the degeneracy of 'modern nobility' was hard to deny. Nobles were losing political authority, selling timber and mining rights on ancestral lands, marrying commoners to repair family fortunes, and on and on. It's easy to see why they might have chosen that moment in history to begin insisting on pedigrees – to ensure that the blood of one English creature, at least, would remain forever pure.

What the *General Stud Book* really did was simple: it made Thoroughbred horses both more valuable and easier to sell. The

Jockey Club could now act as guarantors of provenance, assuring value and estimating authenticity of bloodstock, much as Lloyds of London, a similar loose association of gamblers and wealthy men, stood behind shipping ventures. In 1766, Tattersalls, in Newmarket, held the first Thoroughbred auction. Nobility was for sale, and, as the nobles were delighted to discover, there were buyers. Weatherby's studbook had turned the sport of kings into the liquid and highly speculative business it is today.

EIGHT

The Maiden Run

STUDS MAKE MONEY and mares make babies. This unjust division of labor is hardly restricted to horses, but the retro quality of its sexual politics – the Neanderthal truth of it all – is offset by the fact that, in this case, the babies are for sale. Motherhood, too, has monetary value.

The breeding industry's fixation on the sire is not entirely illogical. In any foal, of course, the influence of sire and dam is equal; each partner contributes exactly 50 per cent of the genetic material. But a mare's reproductive clout is limited by biology, since she can have only one foal a year. A successful sire can have anywhere from a conservative forty (Seattle Slew in his first year back at stud) to more than two hundred foals a year (the aptly named shuttle-stallion Woodman, who routinely sires around a hundred in both the northern and southern hemispheres). When a sire's sons, too, become sires, the numbers – and the resulting genetic influence – can grow to be overwhelming. In the 2000 Breeders' Cup, nearly 90 per cent of the starters had Northern Dancer somewhere in their pedigree. The 'prepotent' sire of sires recreates the breed in his own image.

The large number of foals from each sire makes it possible to generate statistics: lifetime and current-year earnings and something called average-earnings index; the number of two-year-old runners as a subset of all runners; the class, type, and length of races; and so on. These bales of statistics make it possible to turn a series of springtime sexual encounters into a year-round competition. Whether you look at the resulting competition as sport or business, it is competition at its most rudimentary: the winners literally get all the babes.

Turn that equation around, however, and you see what the business is really like: a huge number of mare owners tracking the prepotency of a very limited number of stallions. Mare owners are a fretful bunch. They fret over the fate of their favorite maiden, wondering if she's from a good enough family to make the right sort of match. They lose sleep over some great mare who has only a few more seasons in her and, for mysterious reasons, has never found a partner who could bring out her best qualities. They worry about costs – have they spent enough or too much on her? – and if they have more than one mare, they worry about apportioning their resources so they can see each one settled with the right mate. You'd expect that the author who best expresses the day-to-day spirit of the breeding industry would be Giacomo Casanova; actually, it's Jane Austen.

As in Austen's novels, the value of the family – a thoroughly British concept and one that has nothing to do with family values – is a crucial component in every match. 'Family', like 'class', another term that's often heard in Thoroughbred circles, can be thrown around so confusingly that you often can't tell whether the speaker means to invoke intrinsic qualities, like courage, confidence, and strength, or economic ones, like salability. It's one of the antique assumptions in the Thoroughbred world that the speaker rarely needs to make such a distinction at all.

In horses, 'family' always refers to the female side; half-brothers share a mother, never a father. This tilt is ingrained in the breed, which is founded on the mixing of foreign stallions and local mares, but it is inherent in the horse as well. In a herd of wild horses, nearly every new foal descends from the same stallion, so the question of paternity is unimportant. However, the question of maternity – a foal would phrase that question, 'Who should I run to when I'm hungry or scared?' – is a matter of life and death. Later, as the foal grows stronger and more adventurous and begins to play with other horses, the question takes on subtler shading, and the foal discovers that its place among its playmates is based on the social standing of the mare that it's been running to. If she's the top mare, the one who leads the herd, well, congratulations.

Social standing in the pasture often translates to victory at the track – the foal who can get away with bullying others at the hayrack is often the one who can make it to the winner's circle, too. Success in such cases breeds success, since winning families tend to stay on the farm, while losing families are sold off. This is a simplification, but further investigation still points to the importance of family. One of the most successful broodmare owners I spoke to would occasionally part with mares from a superior family that was getting too numerous. Conversely, he liked to hang on to a few mares from hard-luck families – ones that had 'gone silent' for a generation or so – because he hoped that a currently unpopular line could make a comeback. This made economic sense, because he wound up with a diversified bloodstock portfolio that could withstand the changing fashions of the marketplace. It also made emotional sense. Some of the families had been in *his* family for years and had been good to him and those he loved. It was his turn, he felt, to return the favor.

Every broodmare barn teems with opportunities for this sort of tenderness, and the maternal mood there differs predictably from the lighthearted-jock vibe over at the stallion barn. But don't be distracted by all the cute-foal photo ops. This side of the business is founded on a cruel and basic truth. A colt who doesn't win, no matter what family he comes from, is worth next to nothing, while a mare from a good family retains her value, even if she ran and lost, because she can breed and make babies. That's her job, and it's a job prone to heartbreak and life-and-death emergencies in the middle of the night.

In this mixture of hard work and mortal terror, life in a broodmare barn is like family life anywhere. And since the business, too, must operate on the family model, you won't be surprised to learn that the rewards come unexpectedly, and the payoff for hard work often arrives disguised as luck.

Suzi Shoemaker, of Lantern Hill Farm, is, to use her words, 'super lucky'. In 1982, she spotted a sixteen-year-old pregnant nag, No Crime, selling at the Elmendorf Farm consignment at Keeneland. She knew what she was up against if she wanted to buy her. Shoemaker had gone from bank to bank before, trying to borrow enough for a mare. The problem was this: she was new to the bluegrass, just out of college, and making $125 a week as an assistant farm manager at Manor Brook Farm. The bankers all told her, 'You must be kidding'. But she kept trying, and finally Brien Risk, the big cheese at First National Bank of Nicholasville, who knew her because he handled the Manor Brook accounts, said, 'Look, I know you'll pay it back.' He lent her $20,000.

Twenty thousand was not a tremendous price tag for a horse, but it was a lot for a proven failure whose only previous claim to fame was giving birth, in 1973, in the midst of the Watergate hearings, to an elaborate joke: a filly called Pardon (a pedigree gag: she was out of the No Robbery mare No Crime). Still, Shoemaker was convinced that the folks at Elmendorf, who would go on to win Breeder of the Year that year, must have had some reason to hang on to the mare for so long, so she bought her.

In fact, No Crime had five foals at the track, and within a year of Shoemaker's purchase one of them had become a stakes winner.

That turned the mother into a bona fide property. Shoemaker promptly sold No Crime for $45,000, paid off her loan, and got out of the business, feeling lucky – not because she had bought a horse whose fortunes were on the rise, but because she'd managed to get out of a loan at a time when interest rates were fluctuating between 18 and 20 per cent.

For three years, she stayed out of the business. But then her mother retired and wanted to buy a horse with some extra money she had and Shoemaker helped her. This mare, too, turned a tidy profit. People started to notice.

As she talked about her 'meteoric rise in the horse business' (the ironic punctuation is hers, part of a characteristic, light, self-mocking tone), Shoemaker stood by a paddock fence about a hundred yards from the Victorian house that was both the Lantern Hill office and the Shoemaker residence. There were three barns farther up the farm road, all painted traditional tobacco-barn black, with red roofs, and big tan doors open to reveal the silhouettes of a farrier and groom at work. It was a beautiful hour of the day, with shadows deepening on the hills as the light grew dim, and Shoemaker had stopped her tour to pay a call on Star Empress, a thirty-year-old retired mare. According to Shoemaker, Star Empress had paid for this farm, with the three barns, the grand old house, and the hundred and forty-five acres of pasture in Midway, Kentucky.

Shoemaker is tall, with a lanky disregard for posture and an uncanny resemblance to a TV actress who breezes through complex legal information as if she were in a Noël Coward play. Shoemaker shares this harried conversational style – exam-week insouciance – as well as the oddly sorrowful eyes that, along with the floppy hat she sometimes wears, can give her a look of Chaplinesque poignancy. As we stood by Star Empress, she modestly talked her farm down – it's not a 'secluded paradise' down 'some pristine country lane', but a commercial operation between two very busy roads –

but then she gave in to the romance of it all, explaining how the previous owners, who raised a near Triple Crown winner, Charismatic, turned an old cattle and tobacco farm into a real horse farm.

'Sadie! Come on!' Shoemaker called out, and her dog, a sable-and-white collie, beelined back along the paddock fence with disproportionate enthusiasm. 'Here she comes. Look, she becomes a dog-food commercial.' For a spell, Shoemaker interrupted her life story to play with her dog.

The details of her maneuvers with Star Empress sound a lot like the No Crime caper – horse traders tend to cultivate a talent for a certain type of deal, the way brokers concentrate on a narrow area of expertise, like soy futures, or day traders specialize in a particular strategy, like selling short. In January 1990, Shoemaker (this time with partners, to help spread the risk) bought Star Empress in foal for $45,000; within the year, her two-year-old colt, Star of Gdansk, won a stakes race in Ireland. This rise in fortune allowed Shoemaker to sell the mare's baby, a filly, for $320,000 to a relative of Sheikh Mohammed. But the jackpot didn't stop there: when that filly, Shawgatny, began breeding three years later, Shoemaker bought the filly's first foal, a colt named Brave Charger, for $30,000 at Tattersalls, then resold him in Europe eight months later for about $500,000 – for a total of $745,000 profit (minus feed, vet bills, commissions, and transportation) on Star Empress and her family. 'So she can stay for ever,' Shoemaker said, as the Empress herself walked hesitantly toward the fence. 'If she needs to move in the house, that's fine. I've got a bedroom for her.'

Some spryer mares were keeping the Empress from coming any closer – the 'younger girls', Shoemaker called them, and as they crowded toward her and she rubbed the nose of one and scratched the muzzle of the next, you could see her not so much relax as remember, and become again, the horse-crazy girl she once was, the one who grew up in Springfield Center, New York, riding Morgans and Arabians and winning ribbons on a spotted half-Saddlebred show horse she called Dr Spock. Former horse-crazy girls make up a sizable portion of the workforce in the horse industry, and their presence at every level – as grooms, vets, owners, jockeys, trainers, farm managers, insurance agents – accounts for a certain dream-come-true ambience in the horse world. They do not seem at all surprised to find princes and kings about, as long as there are horses.

No matter how practical such women become, they never seem to abandon their fondness for the books that sustained them in their original euphoria: Walter Farley's *Black Stallion* series, Marguerite Henry's Horseshoe Library (*Misty of Chincoteague*; *Sea Star, Orphan of Chincoteague*), and every other horsey title a girl could get her hands on. This gives the Thoroughbred world a standing army of ironic former bookworms, who, like Shoemaker, seem to enjoy the discrepancy between their old books and the rough and unpredictable present.

Long before she had a farm, Suzi Shoemaker had come up with the name Lantern Hill, in honor of a book she read during this era of her literary education, which is to say fifth grade. *Jane of Lantern Hill*, by L. M. Montgomery, tells a story, full of Dickensian wish-fulfillment, of Jane, an independent young girl, who is packed off to Prince Edward Island, where, in the process of brightening the life of a misanthropic writer (who happens to be her father), she is transformed from an 'awkward, clumsy, stupid' girl into a capable young lady, friend of one and all. During Shoemaker's teenage years, 'Lantern Hill' was the nickname she gave to any place she kept her horse: the affectionate name has grown up with her. 'I've reread the book as an adult,' Shoemaker said, hesitating in much the way that the Empress did as she approached the younger mares. 'And, for its time, it's, um, really an amazingly mature book. I mean, it doesn't make me cringe like I thought it would.'

Shoemaker stood over the paddock fence with her companionable hunch, then shoved away toward the other fields. 'This whole horse thing is supposed to be fun,' she said. 'That's what I remind myself when it gets too tense.'

And why should it get tense?

'Because there's a lot of money involved. And any time there's money involved with anything, you know, it's not fun anymore. But then I step back and say, "Yeah, but look at this. Look at where you live, look at what you do." ' What she was doing just then was walking through the high grass between paddocks as Sadie ran ahead, practicing herding skills on the barren and maiden mares. 'But I know a lot of people for whom it is not fun.'

Jim Snavely is a client of Suzi Shoemaker's, with a maiden mare, Run, that he's looking to breed. Like Shoemaker, Snavely has a good eye for horses, and here is how he got it. He was an accounting professor at the University of Texas at Arlington. And because he had two daughters in grade school, he rented some land down the road and bought a pony. Things just took off from there: pretty soon he'd sold the house in town and bought fourteen acres to go with the horse and two ponies they kept in the back half of the pasture for the kids. That left him the front half to do something with, so he looked around for a couple of quarter-horse mares to produce quarterhorse babies. This was Texas in the sixties, back when they had 'play days' on Friday or Saturday evenings, with timed events for kids and adults where, say, you'd run around barrels. Or you'd ride your horse as fast as you could down to one end, pick up a potato, then come back down to the other end, throw the potato in the bucket. Or you'd take a sword and zoom around a big ring, trying to catch these little rings. And it went all night long, from six o'clock at night to six o'clock the next morning.

The kids would sleep in the back of the station wagon. And about fifteen minutes before it was their turn to ride, at ten or midnight or two AM, Jim or his wife would wake them up, saddle the horse, and put them on it, and the kids would go do their riding and then go back to sleep. The family did this for quite a few years.

Meanwhile, Jim was raising quarterhorses. Some of them he tried to race at the All American Futurity, in Ruidoso, New Mexico, which was a biggie – winner of that race gets a million bucks. Once he had a really nice filly, Paris Pike, who won her trials and ended up winning $900. She was probably about the tenth- or eleventh-best two-year-old filly of the year. And Jim said, 'Now, wait a minute. If I've got that good a *Thoroughbred* filly, you know, I can make lots of money.' So he sold off the quarter horses and shifted over to buying and racing and raising Thoroughbreds.

At this point, the family moved again, to southern Ohio, to be closer to Thoroughbred country, and Jim got a job at Wright State University, in Dayton, where he taught until he retired in 1996. But he didn't get his good eye from being an accounting professor, much as it helped him when he picked up a *Racing Form*. 'What you want to be able to do is to tell a good horse by looking at it,' Jim said. 'And most people cannot do that. In fact, most *trainers* cannot do that. But there are people around – and you can pick them out, they're kind of known – who are really good at picking out good horses. They can look at three thousand and come up with ten of them that are real good ones. And you just have to develop that ability by looking a lot. Now the way I've done it, and I'm pretty good at it – I wouldn't want to say I'm the best, but when I go to the races, and I go to the races a lot, I don't sit upstairs in the dining room or whatnot. I'm always there at the paddock, watching the horses when they saddle them. And you watch them move, and then you watch them race. And you try to see, over a period of time, what do the different breedings look like, when they have a good runner. You know, like, What does a real good Quiet American look like? Because there are only a few of them.'

But here was the problem: Jim's good eye was at war with his good heart. He had one horse in particular, Run, that he could never quite stop worrying about. She was a Canadian-bred filly, 'a fantastic running kind', by Lite the Fuse out of Questelavie, and he bought her for $20,000 just weeks before her half-sister went out and 'run up a storm', winning a Grade I stakes race in New York. 'So I lucked out. And I thought, *Boy, I'm gonna make a ton of money*. And I put Run in a two-year-old-in-training sale down in Florida, and she had a real good work – almost the fastest time of the day. But it made her a little sore in the rear end. So when people come around to look at her she was kinda ouchy or off in the rear end, and they didn't want to spend enough for her. I was gonna let her go if they went eighty, maybe, but I really wanted one hundred thousand. But she didn't go up high enough. So I kept her.

'Anyway, a week later a guy called me down there and he offered me eighty, and I said, "No, I really don't want to sell her." And he called me a week later and offered me a hundred. I told him, "If you'd a done that at the sale you'd've had her, but since I kept her, I really want her." '

Jim got the Canadian trainer Mark Casse to take her. Casse was a good choice because he knew the Ontario tracks where Run, being Canadian bred, was qualified to compete for special purses. Casse also knew Run's family. He and his then wife, Cathy Patton, had trained her dam, Questelavie. In fact, Questelavie had won the Ontario Debutante, a $100,000 stakes race at Fort Erie, on the same day Cathy gave birth to their daughter, Camille. This sort of coincidence is not all that unusual – mention a big race or a record sale, and people like Casse can often cite some personal incident that took place the same day. Skipping back and forth between parallel tracks of experience, between blood and bloodstock, is second nature for horse people, almost an identifying characteristic. And it helps explain why, when Questelavie's filly showed up at his stables, Casse had a good feeling, and he wanted her to do well for reasons that went beyond the obvious.

But from the day he got her, Casse said, Jim had doubts about Run's soundness. 'I thought she had lots of potential and she was fine,' Casse said. 'But you could never convince Jim of that. When we first got her, she was training good, and I kept saying, "Jim, she's doing just fine," and he'd say, "No she can't be." It was always like that.'

Jim told me that Run never did get to be a hundred per cent after her fast work at the sale. He let her race twice, but the second time, right at the starting gate, the jockey heard a loud thunk and he pulled her up. Casse thought the problem could be traced to a ligament that locked up in the hip joint, the sort of complaint an immature horse would outgrow in time. Jim disagreed. 'She just never could get back,' Jim said. 'So I brought her to Kentucky and put her at Suzi's house. And Mark told me, "Now just turn her out for maybe ninety days and put her back in training, and we can race down there in Florida." But I didn't want to do that. I figured that there was a warning there when she came out of the gate. And there was a warning, too . . .' Jim hesitated. 'I lost a filly racing, you know – she died. Before.'

In 1998, Jim Snavely's two-year-old filly Steppes suffered a minor fracture in a race she didn't finish. He withdrew her from training and sent her back to Florida for a layup, but Steppes arrived at the farm with an inexplicable fever that led to her death. Had she been misdiagnosed at the track? Had somebody lost track of her medications? Had she aggravated her injury in transit? No one would ever know. Jim had bought her a few months before for $61,000, more than a man with his eye and spending habits normally had to shell out. But it was not the financial loss that haunted him – he was

STUD

perfectly capable of calculating risk factors and taking writeoffs. If he had to, he could be cavalier about the dangers of racing a colt – but a filly? To lose another filly would break his heart.

And he didn't want to lose Run because, he said, she moved just right. And when she really let loose at the track, she had what they call a nice way of going. 'I mean, if you watch from the rear and from the side, all the legs and the feet and everything go the way they should. Which is kind of rare.' If she could pass these traits on, and Jim Snavely and Suzi Shoemaker could agree on the best stallion at a reasonable price, Run's babies could make them some money. Jim decided to send Run to the breeding shed.

'The truth is,' Casse said, 'I don't really know why Jim retired her. Her soundness wasn't that bad. But Jim had kinda got it in his mind.'

By mid-February 2001, Run had been living under lights for nearly three months. This practice is a relatively simple bit of biological trickery – from December 1, barren and maiden mares are kept in their stalls under a regular 150-watt bulb, venturing outside only during the hours of strongest daylight. The objective is to reset a mare's inner clock, so her body gets the idea that the days are getting longer and she begins to ovulate accordingly, in midwinter – February 14, ideally, right at the start of breeding season – instead of when nature intended, in midspring, when there is a plenitude of tender grass for the newborn foals, who appear on the scene about eleven months after a mare is overcome by the urge to spend a few furtive moments in the company of a prepotent sire.

As a young and developing maiden, Run didn't show strongly encouraging early signs, and the vet, who visited Lantern Hill every day or so to check for such things, didn't think she had enough ovarian activity to qualify for early breeding. But she kept getting visits from 'Storm Cat' – that was the ambitious nickname Shoemaker had bestowed upon her farm's teaser stallion – to see if she began to behave with that impetuous mixture of shyness and lust that marks the onset of the copulatory mood. And sure enough, a week or so after Groundhog Day, Run started indicating that she, at least, was convinced that spring was on its way.

Snavely had wanted to breed Run to a stallion named Siphon, a muscular Brazilian-bred now standing for $20,000 at Airdrie Stud, because he liked the look of Siphon's babies. And he would have sent her to Honour and Glory, who'd won Belmont's Metropolitan Mile in record time, if Coolmore hadn't just jacked up his stud fee, from $15,000 to $40,000. He said, 'I kind of suggested to Suzi, you know, "Let's go breed to some of those more expensive horses." And she said, "No, let's try and make some money." So she was the one that suggested the ten- to fifteen-thousand range. She said, "You can get a good stallion there, and you never know what the first baby's gonna look like." '

It was Shoemaker who first compared the breeding industry with the novels of Jane Austen. 'The whole thing is like a debutante ball, with parents on both sides trying to ensure the most advantageous match,' she wrote in an e-mail update on Run's readiness to breed. 'Weddings arranged by elders solely to advance the fortunes of human families are relatively rare now, but that's exactly the fantasy we're engaged in when we blend two Thoroughbred families.'

The truth is, Shoemaker was touched by Snavely's strong feelings for his winless filly by an unproven sire. When I asked her about the traits that Run was prized for she told me, 'Her biggest claim to fame is her owner's undying love.'

One aspect of Shoemaker's matchmaking that Jane Austen would recognize immediately was the level of raw economic anxiety that motivated the maneuvers. Shoemaker claimed that, contrary to the headlines, most horse breeders were solidly middle-class: she frequently dealt with doctors, lawyers, and former teachers. And that was why she steered Snavely toward Cape Town – the Overbrook stallion who liked to perform alfresco. He was a bargain.

Cape Town, lovably unhurried as a sire, was what breeders call a 'precocious juvenile' at the track, winning his maiden race, a five-furlong sprint at Churchill Downs, just weeks into the two-year-old season, on May 18, 1997 – exactly the sort of early show of force that many breeders believe is the surest predictor of stallion potential. In his three-year-old season, he won two of three prep races on the road to the Kentucky Derby, the Holy Bull Stakes and the Florida Derby, both at Gulfstream Park, and he was in the money at the Toyota Blue Grass Stakes, at Keeneland. After that, he ran twice more, sustaining a career-ending injury in the Preakness, which he did not finish. His record, as he entered stud, was fairly similar to Storm Cat's: early brilliance followed by early retirement.

Cape Town, whose first foals will run in 2002, costs so little largely because Storm Cat costs so much. While the stallion barn may not be the ideal context in which to invoke the principle of trickle-down economics, Storm Cat's tremendous success at stud allows Overbrook to set attractively low stud fees for the rest of its stallions. In fact, with one exception, the stud fees at Overbrook are consistently priced below market, a policy that helps their young studs attract a full book of mares.

I visited Cape Town in the off season, just about the time Snavely was deciding to send Run to him. The stallion complex at Overbrook was bustling with mare owners and bloodstock agents paying calls on potential mates. Kevin Stephens, always so busy tending to mares in the receiving barn from February to June, had enough time now to drive me around the paved roads between the stallion paddocks on a golf cart. 'A breeder may just want to come out and see this horse here,' Stephens said, as we pulled up to Cape Town's two-acre spread. 'But then they're all, "Would it be all right if we just drove past Storm Cat, just so I could say that I saw him?" And these are actual breeders, big-time horse people, you know? Storm Cat, he just has that aurora about him. People want to say, "You know what, I touched that horse. I saw him." '

A Bahamian breeder and his group of family and friends waited by Cape Town's paddock gate while one of the Overbrook grooms trudged out to get him. 'Cape Town won't come to you,' Stephens explained. His conversation had taken on an off-season pace, coming to a full stop between thoughts, as if each sentence were a scene in a play. We sat in the shade of the covered golf cart and watched Cape Town ignoring his approaching groom. 'When you get close to Cape Town, he'll just charge at you like a big rhino. And he won't veer off until he gets right at you. He makes you think you're about to get trampled. And he knows he's doing it. He's real playful. He's just six.' As the hapless groom came closer, Cape Town continued to graze, enjoying the simple pleasures of early retirement. 'Cape Town does not get in no hurry,' Stephens said.

NINE

A Mare in Foal

W HEN R UN ARRIVED at the Overbrook stallion complex
on February 12, she was second in line for the afternoon
session. She waited patiently in her van, betraying no symptoms of
adolescent hormonal overload. Sam Hensley, who had driven her
from Lantern Hill, pointed to a video monitor mounted in the cab
of the trailer which allowed him to keep an eye on Run throughout
the ride. You could see her on the screen, standing serenely, more
like a yoga teacher than a racehorse. 'She's just as nice as she can be,'
he said. 'She ain't even moved.'

On the loading dock, Suzi Shoemaker and Wes Lanter, who had
known each other since their apprenticeships, exchanged remarks
with a lightly barbed *Sonny and Cher Show* mix of insult and
innuendo. Lanter, for example, remarked that he hadn't seen
Shoemaker around the stallion complex lately.

'I got tired of being sent home,' she said, which in the circumstances seemed to impugn either his gallantry or his professionalism.

Lanter chose the latter interpretation. 'I never sent one home. I
cussed a few of them,' he said. 'I've never sent one of yours home.'

Shoemaker gave him a look that seemed to imply that she
recognized a load of horseshit when it was handed to her. Lanter
went on. 'There's a lot of little things you can try before you go to
the needle. I'm a great believer in the ear twitch.' Lanter was
indicating that he usually avoided giving quarrelsome mares a shot

of demosedan ('the needle'), a tranquilizer that makes them more amenable to the advances of the stallion. Instead, he used the ear twitch — a loop of rope at the end of a stick, applied in this case to a mare's delicate ear — as a low-tech alternative. The explanation, however, loses some of the friendly menace of the original.

Banter of this color is almost impossible to avoid around the breeding shed, and Lanter and Shoemaker were being pretty casual about it. Like tennis players feeding each other lobs, they seemed completely unsurprised at what came zinging back.

They changed the subject: a mutual friend, an enthusiastic consumer of bourbon, cigarettes, and two-inch steaks, was refusing to slow down on any front, despite worsening health. 'I expect to get a call,' said Lanter, who seemed to have the most recent news. 'Something I don't want to hear.'

They contemplated mortality for a moment.

'So who do we have today?'

Shoemaker handed over the paperwork — what she'd called the prenup on the drive over. It certified, on the evidence of uterine culture, rectal palpation, and vaginal speculum examination, that Run was clean and sound for breeding. Lanter looked it over and spotted her name. 'So, does she run?'

Shoemaker confessed that the filly was a winless maiden.

'If you named her Stop, she'd probably be a champion,' Lanter said.

The mare before Run was being led, unsuccessfully, out of the breeding shed and back toward an older horse van with a narrow gangplank and the sort of sharp turn into darkness that horses balk at. She came to a dead stop at the bottom of the ramp and the van driver tried pulling her up by her lead shank. The Overbrook team, recognizing an unwinnable standoff, materialized on all sides of the mare, trying at first to coax her gently aboard. Lanter whistled his bird-chirp whistle a few times. One man picked up a handful of gravel and tossed it lightly at the mare's behind. None of these blandishments worked.

Stephens and Lanter locked arms behind her rump and pushed while two other guys pulled at the back of her knees in an attempt to unlock them. The whole gang, hanging on as well as they could, tried to drive the mare forward. The mare kicked backward, missing Stephens's thigh by about a micron. It was a mild day and most of the crew had stripped off their winter coats, so now they were bum-rushing the horse in sweatshirts or green Overbrook jerseys. They seemed to admire the mare and enjoy the effort, glad for the opportunity to measure each other and fine-tune their teamwork this early in the breeding season. ('That's exercise,' Stephens said. 'That's the fringe benefits of the job.') On the third try, the mare started to inch forward; when they got her about halfway up, she apparently realized that very few things in life were worth this much effort and she walked the rest of the way on her own.

Afterward, as the crew walked back to the receiving barn to get ready for Run, Lanter explained the general admiration for the mare. 'We always assume, if the mare kicks, that she's not right. This mare was fighting, but she was right.' He sat on a chair in the barn and Stephens pressed the button to open the divider between the teaser stallion and Run. 'Mares have bad days, too.'

Shoemaker stood outside the barn – the copper flashing on the Overbrook roofs interfered with cell-phone reception – calling a friend she'd asked to put in the first few bids on a horse she was selling at an auction crosstown. He could stop, she told him, once the bidding got past $4,500. This is a common way for the seller to establish a reserve price. Lanter rested on a chair – he'd strained his knee in January, trying to shoulder Cat Thief into proper position on a test mare – and watched today's teaser stallion, Countercheck, doing his work with Run.

Countercheck was smoother than the average teaser stallion,

perhaps because he had the pedigree for it: his dam was Swift Reply, by He Loves Me out of Swift Response, and his paternal grandam was the unraced Sex Appeal. He seemed to operate with a suave economy of gesture and a minimum of macho noise, and Run apparently went for his rap. 'She's winking,' an Overbrook groom reported from a rearward position.

With the preliminaries out of the way, Run was led to the padded chute where Stephens would wrap her tail and wash her. She looked fresh, 'just like new money', Stephens said. 'We have the mares come in all combed and pretty. And Storm Cat, he'll come down all caked with mud. And the mares leave with dirt on their back.'

Run's behavior was bearing out everything Snavely'd said about her. The retired professor had called her the best filly – the best horse – he'd ever owned, describing her as 'really smart' and a fast learner with great attitude. To evaluate a horse, farmers often use the same practical criteria that primary-school teachers use on children; negative accomplishments, like lack of misbehavior, can get far more praise than they deserve. But Run's composure – she was remarkably unruffled by her adventures in the breeding shed – seemed to have deeper origins than brute obedience. She seemed modest, easy, and unaffected, and yet when she entered a room (a barn, a breeding shed), she gave off a Jackie O sense of quiet entitlement. You liked being around her. You felt that good things were about to happen.

Perhaps Lanter was responding to this remarkably mature quality when he double-checked with the man who'd unloaded Run to verify that she was, in fact, a maiden.

He was told yes. She was indeed.

'And she's a shy maiden,' Lanter said, as he prepared the farm's largest breeding roll – fitting a plastic glove over the bolster cushion that softens the impact of the well-endowed stud. Cape Town entered the shed, and almost immediately he walked over to Run and began to exhibit what is called the Flehman response, a peculiar animal reaction that stallions go through in response to the smell of the genitals and the hormone-rich urine of a mare in heat. Cape Town extended his neck and curled back his lips, remaining in this position for several seconds. Nobody is quite sure what this elaborate gesture accomplishes (the textbooks say 'behavioral urinalysis', and recent studies suggest pheromone sampling), but, like all gestures of connoisseurship, it comes off as remarkably self-involved and, no matter how discreet the stallion is in its indulgence, he manages to exclude everybody else present: imagine Orson Welles sitting alone at the best table in the restaurant, tasting his mouthful of Chianti with all the theatrical bubbling of the oblivious wine lover.

Since it was so early in the season, Cape Town didn't require any of the elaborate scene-setting or extra helping hands that he needs later in the spring, once the procession of winking fillies has grown to be oh so everyday. After he'd considered Run's bouquet, he prepared to move on to her body, rearing and roaring and coming down upon her as far as the cushion would allow.

'Come on, Capey. Step up.'

They cheered him on, and for a moment it seemed as if Cape Town might have acquired a more professional attitude over the off season. But before the idea could gain plausibility, the sophomore stallion reverted to form and fell back to the ground. Lanter stepped away. Folks returned to idle conversation: 'Who was the better Catwoman, Julie Newmar or Michelle Pfeiffer?' The breeding-shed phone rang and Doc Yocum answered: 'Stallions.'

Run remained silent and unmoving through all this, as if she were the experienced one. At one point, she checked behind her, turning as far as she could with her upper lip in a twitch. Cape Town was lost in whatever constitutes thought in a horse. But soon enough, the patience of the stallion handlers was rewarded: he started in again with the stretching neck and the curling lip. Unfortunately, his second effort ('Come on, Cape. Come on – Aw, don't give up the ghost') ended as inconclusively as his first.

Eventually, the comedy came to a close: on the third go, Cape Town did what he was paid to do. When Lanter washed him off in the aftermath, the water ran red.

'Suzi,' Lanter said, giving the medical report as Shoemaker walked back to her car, 'she tore a little bit but it was right up the suture.' When they go to the track, maiden mares have their labia sewn shut, so that vigorous exercise won't fill the vagina with air, causing infections and potential infertility. It was hard to tell whether the bleeding could be traced to Run's loss of her maidenhead or to Cape Town's prodigiousness, but whatever the source of the injury, Run, as usual, remained unflustered.

Afterward, I asked Shoemaker how she thought it went. 'Oh, she was a model citizen,' she said. 'I've been at some other farms where it was like rape. There'd be five guys hanging off the mare. And she'd have a leg in the air and a twitch and she'd be drugged. I remember thinking, "And I got into this because I love horses?" '

When your cash flow depends on the reproductive health of the Thoroughbred mare, you will often discuss the following items in business meetings: infertility, venereal disease, hormone imbalance, abortions (both spontaneous and elective), cervical or uterine 'incompetence', and a range of fetal malpresentations (breech, dog-sitting, flexed capri, wryneck, and so on) that represent an immediate threat to your ability to collect on your investments. Often, one of the parties at such a business meeting will have his hand lodged some two and a half feet up the rear end of a horse. It is surprising how quickly this comes to seem normal.

I have had many pleasant conversations with veterinarians in just such circumstances. We discussed a great variety of things – the Egyptian collection at the Chicago Art Museum, Nietszche, euthanasia, college wrestling, the proximity of Times Square hotels to various Broadway shows – but the conversation almost always returned to the topic at hand. 'The horse is the single most amazing species for the number of hormones that are produced in their urine,' Jeanne Bowers told me, on a beautiful spring day at the Harris Ranch, in Coalinga, California. 'They can stop labor! And they're the only species that can do that. Essentially, they decide whether they're going to have the baby or not. And the hormonal mechanisms that are involved are so complex. They are the single most fascinating reproductive species outside of the arctic seal.'

The plentiful hormones in the urine of a pregnant mare form the active ingredient in Premarin (*Pre*gnant *Ma*re U*rine*), the best-selling estrogen-replacement pill, and one that provides the basis for an entire industry whose raw material (along with the fascinating sexuality of the arctic seal) we shall leave for other writers to discuss. Still, there are great economic incentives for plumbing the mysteries of the mare's reproductive system, and veterinary science more than keeps pace with advances in human reproductive technology in matters such as cloning, embryo transfer, and fertility drugs.

But some things remained cloaked in mystery no matter what species you deal with. For instance, no one seemed to know the physiological purpose of the mare's clitoris – an unmistakable appendage, the size of a Brazil nut, which all that winking seemed designed to expose. Suzi Shoemaker gave me the most fully imagined hypothesis, that the forceful but brief stimulation from the stallion led to increased uterine contraction that was, perhaps, functional (there's a lot of internal-suction-based physics going on at that juncture). It was a practical theory and it seemed to leave enough wiggle room to allow for a pleasure principle.

One veteran vet had no leads on function, but he did have

surgical experience. 'In 1977 and '78, we had a disease that came in here from Ireland and France called contagious equine metritis,' he said. 'It's a venereal disease. And one of the places that we found it was in the clitoral sinus. Most of us didn't even know there was a clitoral sinus, you know. It's a very small little area. So we had to start culturing that area and for quite a few years we had to remove the clitoris before the mare could come in from Europe. I made a trip to France to show veterinarians how to do it once.'

Kentuckians like to boast about their highly concentrated population of Thoroughbred horses, but there is a downside: disease can spread so rapidly in the bluegrass that infection rates can reach epidemic levels before the problem is even detected, let alone diagnosed. Naturally, an industry founded on the sexual act is especially vulnerable to venereal disease. The 1978 outbreak of contagious equine metritis (which causes infertility or early abortion) was followed in 1984 by an outbreak of equine viral arteritis, an upper respiratory infection (that also causes abortion) spread by contact with infected semen or airborne droplets (for example, those produced by the cough of an afflicted horse).

But a disease doesn't have to be venereal to cripple the breeding industry. In 2001, in the months when most of the live covers chronicled here took place, many Thoroughbred mares suffered a mysterious and devastating syndrome. Those in the first months of pregnancy were absorbing their foals; those in the final stages were aborting. The early foal loss hit maiden mares first and hardest. But, because maidens normally suffer a higher miscarriage rate than older mares, it took slightly longer for the problem to reach detectable levels, and the value of the warning was nearly lost.

Late-term abortions were harder to miss. On May 4, on the eve of the Kentucky Derby, Hagyard Davidson and McGee's emergency unit admitted fourteen 'red-bag' foals – deliveries in which the inflamed placenta, or 'red bag', precedes the foal, a condition that frequently results in the foal's asphyxiation during birth. On Derby Day itself, the veterinary clinic registered its highest one-day total of foals and fetuses brought in for necropsy – seventy-three. Four days later, the University of Kentucky's Livestock Disease Diagnostic Center had recorded 346 aborted foals or stillborn fetuses for the season, an increase of 700 per cent over normal figures. Everybody knew there was a problem, but nobody knew how it started or even what to call it.

What they did know was that it had been a strange spring. In early April, temperatures hit the eighties and stayed there for days. Midsummer weather was followed by a week of winter: snowfall and several nights of hard frost. But after April 17, nothing fell from the sky for weeks, and the drought continued well into May. That wasn't all. Eastern tent caterpillars, whose population normally rises and falls on a ten-year cycle, had grown so numerous that spring that some farms kept brooms by the barn doors to sweep a path through the carpet of caterpillars whenever they walked outside.

The catalogue of symptoms grew – live foals were having trouble breathing; young mares developed eye infections; yearlings and older horses suffered severe heart trouble; the miscarrying mares had levels of residual progesterone, the active contraceptive ingredient in the Pill, which rendered most of them infertile for the rest of the breeding season – and the scramble to find a cause began. Some suggested that an obscure fungus, or mycotoxin, that thrived under April's unusual weather conditions had somehow managed to coat the bluegrass. Some blamed an old culprit: fescue grass, a sort of imitation bluegrass, which contains an endophyte believed to disturb hormone levels and cause abortions. And many researchers focused on the caterpillars, who have a gift for happily munching the poisonous leaves of the native black cherry tree and then, a little while later, excreting cyanide on the pasture grass.

Each unproven theory required separate measures to combat its conjectured effects. To avoid mycotoxins, breeders brought horses out of the pasture and into the stables – a risky proposition, since it limited exercise and thus endangered the pregnancies of even healthy mares. To protect against fescue toxicity, broodmare managers pumped the mares full of domperidone. This drug, often given to mares as they approach their due date, to stimulate milk production, was thought to reduce damage caused by grazing the fescue. And even though the Eastern tent caterpillars had moved into their cocoons by the time the cyanide-poisoning theory was put forth, some breeders went out anyway and started chopping down the cherry trees that sprout like weeds between paddocks.

Dealing with the immediate crisis was costly; most mares, even those thought to be unaffected, had to receive emergency treatments (frequent shots, extra sonograms, and a slew of dietary supplements) that added an average twenty-five dollars a day to the cost of keeping a horse – more than it costs to keep a mare in the first place. But the extra maintenance costs were nothing compared to the potentially devastating long-term losses. According to John Gaines, the founder of Gainesway, who wrote about the crisis in an editorial in *The Blood-Horse*, a late-term abortion meant an average of $116,000 lost revenue: the farm would miss $13,000 in boarding fees, the stallion owner a $15,000 stud fee, and the mare owner $88,000 for a horse it would not sell. Most Thoroughbred owners, like Jim Snavely, kept five mares or fewer. Gaines claimed that nearly two-thirds of owners had household incomes of less than $75,000. Even a single abortion could run these players out of the business.

Mare reproductive loss syndrome, as the blight came to be called, often acted capriciously, like a tornado, taking 50 per cent of the foal crop on one farm and leaving a neighboring farm untouched. But one thing was certain: it hit small farms hardest, and their hardship was passed on to the small businesses that depended on them –

blacksmiths, feed suppliers, landscapers, tack salesmen, van drivers. The crisis exposed a side of the breeding industry that the public was not accustomed to seeing: its middle class.

After a few weeks of heavy losses, the rate of both early foal loss and late-term abortion had returned to near normal levels. Breeders (and the pasture scientists and epidemiologists who advised them) assumed that a series of hard rains, from May 18 to May 24, had cleansed the fields of any residual contamination from the caterpillar or mycotoxin. The syndrome vanished as mysteriously as it appeared, and breeders began to take a tally of the damage.

On his first live cover back in the breeding shed after his spinal surgery, the ever fertile Seattle Slew 'settled' Dreams of Success and the four-year-old filly kept her pregnancy through her sixty-two-day checkup on April 16. But three weeks later, just after the worst of the weather, she lost her foal, and she didn't go back in heat in time to return to the breeding shed. Dreams of Success suffered the fate so many maidens did in 2001; her produce record will show that in her first season as a broodmare she was barren.

Despite her early ambivalent signs of ovulation, Run got in foal on her first visit to Cape Town and kept in foal through her thirty-nine-day checkup. But by her next checkup, in late April, she too had miscarried. Shoemaker believed that Run's miscarriage occurred well before the strange weather and plague of caterpillars and mycotoxins hit the bluegrass. Jim Snavely's favorite filly had lost her foal for the same reason that most maiden mares do: she was immature. It was another lucky break for Shoemaker – Run was 'empty' during the worst of the blight, and because she lost her foal so early, she went back in heat quickly and returned to Overbrook in early May. She was still pregnant when *Stud* went to press.

TEN

Stud in a Box

T HE COUNTRY'S MOST successful Standardbred breeding farm, Hanover Shoe Farms, sends out a lot of FedEx packages, mostly 50-cc shipments of cooled semen, in plastic syringes packed in climate-controlled Styrofoam boxes made by Equine Express II. The charge for such a shipment is anywhere from $3,000 (for Ball and Chain, a pacer) to $20,000 (for Western Hanover, a champion pacer whose children have earned well over a hundred million dollars). The semen is collected by three veterinarians, Allison Kaufman, Jacqueline O'Donnell, and Bridgette Jablonsky, who runs the farm, and is known as Dr J.

Dr J is not a native of the Pennsylvania countryside. She comes from Syosset, Long Island, and she grew up on a farm just off the Jericho Turnpike that boarded pacers and trotters from the old Roosevelt Raceway. Much as she loves Hanover Shoe Farms, sometimes she wishes it were in New Jersey, where there is occasionally something to do. Instead, she lives in a seventy-five-year-old wooden house about fifty yards from the stallion barn that the night watchman visits every hour. She has no privacy. But she doesn't really need it, she points out, since Hanover, Pennsylvania, is not the guy capital of the world.

Dr J is not exactly a complainer, but her accent and the dark roots of her blond hair go with a certain sarcastic, gum-cracking grouchiness that Long Island is famous for. Her biggest swear word, for example, is 'freakin'. It's a wonder she doesn't use it over lunch, where, despite the fact that everybody knows she's on a ruthless diet, she still has to endure a long and explicit conversation about fancy food at Manhattan restaurants, in the presence of her boss, the Hanover president, Jim Simpson, and the farm PR guy, Murray Brown. To top it all off, Brown tells a story about Dr J's family, and how they changed their name after coming over from Poland, from 'Jablon' to 'Jablonsky', and not the other way around, because they thought 'Jablonsky' sounded more American.

'That's the sole reason I wanted to get married – to change that name. And now it's too late,' Dr J says. 'Even if I do get married, I can't change all my professional licenses.'

Jim Simpson, a fifth-generation horseman, and the third gen- eration of Simpsons in charge of the farm, tells her that she'll have to date to get married. Then Brown reminds Dr J that she *is* married: 'You're married to your horses.'

'It's true.' Dr J tries to curl her lip in disgust, but it doesn't quite work, and she ends up fighting off a smile. 'On Jackie's desk she has her wedding picture. On Allison's desk she has her wedding picture. And on my desk is a head shot of The Panderosa.' In the picture, Dr J is, in fact, hugging The Panderosa, a yearling she worked for hours to save, while his mother, Daisy Harbor, struggled and died in delivery.

Simpson says he can remember a time when women weren't allowed into the breeding sessions. Now they're running the farm, top to bottom. 'They're better than guys, for the most part. More conscientious, more caring. Invariably, when you hire a couple – I've found this at the race stable, the training stable – the woman is the anchor and does all the work and the guy's a drunk or a druggie or a wife beater. That's still the case.'

Dr J thinks that stallions respond better to women. 'Because the more rough you get with stallions, the more rough the stallion gets with you. You have to be able to find a happy medium, and a woman's more likely to do that.'

The restaurant, Buona Fortuna, is the new pasta place in what the chamber of commerce would probably call downtown Hanover: a few streets (Chestnut, Broadway, Poplar, Elm) of solid German-looking brick buildings, filled with hobby shops, Tharp's barbershop (with a sign in the window advertising house calls), W.E. Sell Sporting Goods store, and Famous Hot Wieners grill. As Dr J heads back to work, the lunch-hour bustle of downtown is quickly replaced by quiet residential streets – wooden homes flying the flags of Dale Earnhardt and the Baltimore Ravens – which in turn quickly yield to the surrounding jumble of antique farmland and lonely new subdivisions.

Much of the open land belongs to Hanover Shoe Farms, whose holdings are a patchwork of separate plots acquired over the decades from local Standardbred breeders as they got out of the business. Dr J has to crisscross Hanover to do her job, driving, for example, out of the side streets right into an old county fair-ground, past a grand and out-of-service Standardbred track (although racing ended here decades ago, race meets at county fairs still make up a good chunk of the Standardbred season) to a broodmare barn from 1950, with dusty mullioned windows and vintage wooden stalls. 'One of the most beautiful horse barns you'll ever see,' Dr J says.

After that, she follows a local highway back to a farm everyone calls Fatty's (although nobody can remember who Fatty was), stopping her Hanover Shoe SUV at another old and picturesque barn. This one has peeling wooden walls painted a butterscotch color, and it's laid out like an Italian villa, with the stalls facing in, so the maiden and barren mares look over their stall doors onto an empty grass square, now swept with snow. Dr J has come to Fatty's to certify the mares that are ready for breeding – double-checking the morning work of the teaser stallion – and the grooms lead the maidens to her one by one.

Dr J is just shy of five feet tall, so she has to stand on a stool to perform the palpations. At most big farms, this sort of work is done with a hand-held sonogram device, but Dr J has too many mares to bother with the slow and cumbersome machine. She finds it faster and more accurate to do it the old-fashioned way, checking every animal by hand. As we chat, she puts some Vet Lube on a plastic glove and reaches up the rectum to feel around the mare's ovaries – checking for the follicles, which swell just before ovulation and then soften to about the size and firmness of a ripe apricot. This is the optimum time to inseminate a mare, about twelve hours or so before the follicle releases its egg. Palpation is an athletic process, requiring strength and a feathery touch, and she rises onto her toes and scrunches her face in a mixture of physical effort and diagnostic calculation.

From time to time, her job requires her to perform an abortion in this position. For example, when a mare has twins, it's standard practice to abort one as soon as possible – ideally, within twenty days of conception, when the abortion can still be performed manually, a process called pinching off – so that the surviving foal will grow to full size. 'Oh yeah,' she says, 'I get very muscular on my right side' – her palpating side – 'and my hands are so small that I have to feel one side of the follicle and then the other. A man could just pick the whole thing up. But then, my hands are so small that I can isolate one twin and pinch it off.'

After checking maidens, Dr J gets back in her truck and heads out to Elmer Farm to visit Melon Hanover, a thirteen-year-old mare whose cervix was torn up delivering a foal with a contracted leg. Even though Melon can no longer carry a foal to term, she's a consistent mare who's far too valuable to retire. So each year, Dr J oversees an embryo transfer – a procedure that is not allowed in

Thoroughbreds, but is fairly routine practice with Standardbreds. To perform the transfer, the farm has to have at least three recipient mares synchronizing their cycles with Melon's, ready to take the fertilized egg once she's successfully bred.

This seems to be a sore topic with Melon. As far as she's concerned, she's through with the birthing business. When Dr J comes into her stall, Melon turns her butt away and kicks a plank on the wall. But the good doctor is not easy to intimidate; she puts her stool down behind the mare and pulls out the Vet Lube. 'She's got her quirks,' Dr J says fondly. 'You should have seen her when she was younger. She was terrible.'

Standardbreds are a nineteenth-century American invention, bred to race in harness on a stretch of country road. They're sturdier than Thoroughbreds, being smaller with heavier bones, and a good one can race nearly every week and be none the worse for it. Standardbred times are slower than Thoroughbreds' over equal distances, but much of the difference can be attributed to the difficult Standardbred gaits − trotting or pacing − which the horses must maintain throughout a race. In trotting, the opposite legs (right front and back left, left front and back right) work together in a gait that's natural in a dog but takes some training for a horse; a trotter at full speed looks upright but full of hustle, like a commuter with a coffee cup racing for an empty seat on the train. In pacing, the legs on one side of the body move together, and the horse runs with a pretty, bounding scissor step. About 80 per cent of Standardbred races today are for pacers only, which means that most harness races have the long-legged tippy-toe look of ballet.

Harness racing made the transition from county-fair attraction − the bob-tailed nag of 'Camptown Races' fame was a Standardbred − to big-city sport in 1940, when George Morton Levy, a New York trial lawyer, opened Roosevelt Raceway on Long Island, and offered racing under lights. He introduced a rolling starting gate in 1946 (eliminating the need for so many boring restarts) and by 1953, as the Eisenhower economic boom took off, Roosevelt Raceway was getting a nightly turnout of twenty thousand racing fans. Other big cities took notice and soon lighted tracks began attracting bettors throughout the Northeast and Midwest.

The Standardbred foundation sire was Hambletonian, born on May 5, 1849, in Orange County, New York, the result of the mating of a Thoroughbred sire and a Norfolk trotter dam. He was a muscular horse, with a butt that rode higher than his shoulders – the so-called trotting pitch. His best descendants could all run a mile, hitched to a sulky, in less than two and half minutes; this was the original standard a horse had to meet to be called Standardbred. Hambletonian had 1,331 children in his career at stud, and every stallion in the Hanover Shoe Farms barn – essentially, every Standardbred in the world – descends from this one Yankee sire.

Today almost all the siring in the breed is done by artificial insemination. The practice is so widespread that virtually every top Standardbred stud will die a virgin in the technical sense – which, as any teenage boy or Arkansan president will testify, is the only sense that counts. At Hanover Shoe Farms, no effort is made to enrich the sensual life of the stallions by offering them the real thing on occasion, partly because the experience might ruin their careful training (stallions are not naturally excited by the presence of the pommel horse, the sturdy padded device they mount during a collection procedure) and partly because mares kick. No stallion manager would risk losing years of steady income for something as frivolous and fleeting as sexual fulfillment – an important lesson that's far easier to apply to other species than to one's own.

Artificial insemination offers many advantages. Transmission of venereal disease is all but eliminated (even in those cases where the pathogenic agent is transmitted by the semen, the smaller volume used in AI lessens risks, which may be further reduced by antibiotics added to the sample). The threat of injury is significantly decreased – stallions are in no danger of encountering an uncooperative mare, mares are under no threat of being savaged, and fewer people get hurt. Poor or injured breeders can continue to produce: the mare who can't bear the weight of the stud, the stallion who can't rear up. Since every sample can be divided many times, AI prevents overuse of the stallions: top Standardbreds, who produce more offspring than their Thoroughbred peers, actually breed far less often, so they're not worn out by the annual rush of clients, all those maidens and barren mares carefully brought into estrus at the beginning of the breeding season. That's the sort of heavy workload that, some Kentucky breeders say, can threaten a Thoroughbred's health and lessen his fertility.

Advantages like these made AI the standard procedure for Standardbreds long before advances in shipping and handling allowed breeding farms to fly sperm across the country. Until recently, mares still had to be vanned to Standardbred breeding farms like Hanover Shoe, where they were bred on the grounds by artificial insemination. But since the advent, in the eighties, of Equitainers (bulky blue thermos bottles about the size of a fire extinguisher) and, in the nineties, the lighter Styrofoam boxes made by ExpectaFoal, Bio-Flite, and Equine Express II, mare owners in distant states have been able to order semen over the phone as soon as a local vet determines that their mare is ready to ovulate. Today, the transport of semen (cooled, not frozen, since more sperm survive cooling than freezing) is the industry norm – and for some threatened breeds, like the Exmoor pony, shipped semen is their only means of survival. There are only eight fertile Exmoor stallions in North America; thanks to Bio-Flite, et al., they can service mares in Ontario, Nova Scotia, California, and Virginia.

Surprisingly, there isn't much debate about artificial

insemination. Standardbred breeders aren't likely to abandon the practice and Thoroughbred breeders aren't likely to take it up. For each group, the established method is a rule of the game, and it's only beginners who argue about the rules.

Dr J has no interest in plying her trade at a Thoroughbred farm; her game is Standardbreds. As we walk through the stallion barn, though, she indulges the newcomer and discusses the differences between the two breeds. 'Thoroughbreds tend to be finer,' she says, 'but with more massive bodies. They're much more muscular horses. And they have these little fine legs and prettier heads.' You can hear each valiant attempt to be impartial turning into subtle insult – her tone implies that the fine legs are too breakable, the pretty heads contain no common sense. It's clear that Standardbred horses are her favorite company. And among Standardbreds, she likes the stallions best of all.

The aesthetic at Hanover Shoe Farms is practical; Standardbreds are cheaper than Thoroughbreds, and very few owners are sheikhs or billionaires. (Earlier in the day, just to show me that 'it's not only Thoroughbred owners who are big shots', Dr J pointed out Veronica Lake, a seven-year-old bay mare who was owned by Alan Kirschenbaum, producer of *Yes, Dear* and *Coach*.) Most owners value Standardbred horses for their durability and reliable earning power, and the grounds at Hanover Shoe seem to reflect those virtues. In late February, the place looks like Andrew Wyeth country: barren, cold, honest – hardy and endangered all at once. Jim Simpson acknowledged the plainness, and he told a story about a job applicant, fresh from the bluegrass, who expressed disappointment at this lack of style. The plainspoken owner at the time, L. B. Sheppard, replied, 'Boy, in Kentucky they raise fences. Here we raise horses.'

The one grand exception to the bottom-line design is the stallion barn, which is sunny and spacious, loaded with cigar-colored hardwood and trimmed with brass. Even Storm Cat doesn't get the space these studs enjoy. As she walks down the row of stallions, Dr J speaks with a mixture of reverence and access, like a Senate tour guide. She stops at Lindy Lane – the leading first-year trotting sire, and one of the four stallions she collects faithfully – who's standing in his stall, knee deep in straw, munching away drowsily and staring out toward the open fields. 'He's never done anything since he's been here to indicate he'd be athletic,' she says. 'But if you saw him race – He didn't know the meaning of the word "quit".' Lindy Lane is one of very few fertile sons of the popular but mostly infertile sire, Valley Victory, and Lindy gets a lot of his father's turn-away business.

She stops next at Sierra Kosmos, a long-faced horse who has a blaze on his forehead and heavy-lidded eyes with the upward cast of the martyr. Like Lindy Lane, he's a trotting sire – that is, his sons and daughters have a natural gift for the difficult gait. But unlike Lindy Lane, Sierra Kosmos is related to nobody important; he might as well have come from Kazakhstan. This allows Hanover Shoe Farms to offer mare owners a trotting sire for any occasion. If you want to inbreed – and thus intensify the hereditary effect of a prized forebear – Hanover has the highly pedigreed Lindy Lane. On the other hand, if you want an outcross, to give fresh blood to your bloodstock, they have Sierra Kosmos.

Dr J has already introduced me to these two stallions in earlier conversations, at other barns. When she was looking over newborn foals that morning, she held a little filly who squealed as Dr J tried to tag her. 'There you go,' Dr J said. 'Lindy Lane.' Apparently, that squeal is one of the most dominant characteristics in any Lindy Lane foal, and she promised me that I would hear it again – mocking, angry, high-pitched, a real banshee screech – in the breeding shed. 'We know who *your* daddy is,' Dr J said to the feisty newborn. 'We don't have to DNA-type you.'

She'd first spoken of Sierra Kosmos while checking on a pregnant mare who'd had difficulty bringing her foals to term. The mare had been bred to Sierra Kosmos because Dr J believes that mares don't abort his foals as readily as some other sires'. 'There's no scientific basis for it,' she says. 'It's just a feeling I get, having been exposed to it so much. If we can breed a mare to a couple of different stallions, she'll abort, or it'll be born dead. But it seems like his foals are more hardy in the womb, and they have a greater chance of having life once they are born.'

Actually, she tends to speak more freely about the stallions when she isn't in their presence. When we reach Big Towner, Dr J pauses at the stall door and says simply, 'Nobody would mistake him for a Thoroughbred.' He's short, slim, brown, long-bodied, and old – the same age as Seattle Slew. A plaque beside his stall notes that Big Towner's children – all 1,942 of them, an average of 97 for every year at stud – have earned more than $101 million at the track. (Seattle Slew's 931 progeny, by comparison, have chalked up only $53 million – only slightly more per capita, but far less overall.)

But in the broodmare barn, out of earshot, she spoke freely about Big Towner's problems. 'He's twenty-seven. He doesn't like to breed,' she said that morning. And if he has to go to the breeding shed on consecutive days, 'the horse just won't do it. And there's nothing we can do to make him do it'. So if they have a little left over from the day before – technicians can add semen extender, basically chemically enriched skim milk, and divide the average sample into as many as fifteen portions – they'll give a mare owner that. 'And we'll say, "Here. It's not fresh, but at least we're giving you something." Every time I get him' – by which Dr J means every time she succeeds in collecting a sample from the reluctant sire – 'I celebrate, because he just doesn't want to do it. He's had enough.'

On the day of my visit, Dr J is working out of a crowded office that she shares with her fellow vets, Allison Kaufman and Jacqueline

O'Donnell, and that day there are two big topics of conversation. One is how to decorate the place after the renovation – O'Donnell and Kaufman keep mentally moving the desks around, and putting in phone lines, and improving on the window treatments, which isn't hard, since all they have up is venetian blinds that seem to date from the same low point in the Carter era as the wood-paneled walls and the mud-splattered white linoleum underfoot.

The other big topic is Honcho, the farm's much maligned teaser stallion. ('What are you talking about?' Kaufman asks. 'I thought you used the words "Honcho" and "excellent" in the same sentence.') Dr J says Honcho has a little side business, inseminating nurse mares. Nurse mares are lactating mares of less expensive breeds rented seasonally to provide milk whenever a birth mother dies in delivery or rejects her foal – the latter is a fairly frequent occurrence among high-strung Thoroughbreds, a little less so among the more even-tempered Standardbreds. Nurse mares must be returned pregnant, as part of the rental agreement, and that's the marketing niche that Honcho's owner is aiming to exploit.

'He gets like two mares a year, and we don't have an AV,' Dr J says. An AV is an artificial vagina. The AV that Standardbreds use differs significantly from the model your next-door neighbor ordered from the Hypatia Lee website, which goes to great lengths to be as lifelike as possible. The Standardbred's simply goes to great lengths: it's between sixteen and twenty-two inches long, made of latex, and shaped like a sleeve. A stoppered valve in the outer surface of the sleeve allows it to be filled with about five pounds of water, which is heated to 130 degrees, about as hot as the sex organs of a mare in heat. The artificial vaginas come in various styles – Colorado, Roanoke, Japanese, Polish, French, and so on. Hanover Shoe Farms prefers the Missouri model, because it's light and maneuverable and because it allows for additional stimulation, since it's open at both ends. Each stallion has his own. But the farm doesn't keep extras lying around. 'Do we have any really old AVs?' Dr J asks. 'I don't want to use any of the stallions'.'

Each of the women has a roster of stallions that they collect. O'Donnell always takes Sierra Kosmos and Arturo; Kaufman gets Western Hanover and Ball and Chain; and that leaves Dr J with Lindy Lane, Big Towner, the young stallion Dragon Again, and The Panderosa – 'just because I really like him'. They stay with the same stallions because routine is good for horses, who are not creatures who yearn for variety in their sex life. Their love of routine is so strong that sometimes just spotting a vet in the breeding shed can arouse them. This sort of transference, which might be awkward in any other context, makes the job easier. Of course, with experience, the vets pick up a few tricks, the little things each one of their stallions likes and dislikes, and that makes the job easier, too.

But nobody's assigned to Honcho, and apparently Dr J is in no mood to take him on, mostly because of his unusual postcoital habit. To inform whoever ends up with him of the potential danger, she makes a general announcement: 'The worst thing he'll do is faint when he's done.'

My portion in the general laughter that follows is muted because, like it or not, I identify with the teaser stallions, whose job descriptions have a more knockaround, real–life quality. It's hard not to sympathize with Honcho, but this stirring of sympathy gives the merriment a surreally personal quality, as if I'd just been thrown back into high school and forced to listen to the conversation I always imagined taking place, out in the parking lot, among the girls who smoked.

'Has he really done that?' O'Donnell asks.

'Yeah,' Dr J says. 'He kinda just slides off. You just got to be on your toes. Just get out of his way. He's a gentleman, though. He's a very nice horse.' Ah, poor Honcho: the likable sort.

Luckily, conversation quickly turns to the foals that come of

Honcho's little side business, and what happens to them when the nurse mare gets rented out the following year. Dr J says the owner of the nurse mare raises the Honcho foal 'by bucket' (that is, putting everything the foal eats in a bucket). O'Donnell is more idealistic. She hopes that the two foals, both the lowly Honcho foal and the expensive Standardbred foal destined to take a turn under the bright lights of the racetrack, will be raised together, like Romulus and Remus, socializing and suckling from the same teat.

The breeding shed at Hanover Shoe Farms is laid out very differently from the ones in Kentucky. At Overbrook or Three Chimneys or Claiborne Farm, the emphasis is on the act of breeding, and the shed is a bare, spacious stage for the brutal theatrics of the live cover. The vet and the stallion manager operate their technical equipment – a microscope or two, a video monitor recording the proceedings, a computer with a spreadsheet program to keep track of the breedings – in a clean, small room off in the wings. At Hanover Shoe Farms, the proportions are nearly reversed, and the vets' room, with its cabinetful of AVs, multiple sinks, high-powered microscopes feeding video hookups, SpermaCue machine giving digital readouts of sperm count by the billion, curettes, fusettes, test tubes, counters lined with bottles of extender, and stainless-steel refrigerators filled with packets of fresh product waiting for pickup, is the busy center of activity. The work of the stud is what takes place offstage, a solitary prelude to the science that follows.

Before the stallions arrive, the vets busy themselves prepping the AVs. Western Hanover, one of the leading sires of the previous year, is scheduled first, so Allison Kaufman, who has the stallion on her collection roster, runs hot water in the sink. She holds a candy thermometer to give her a readout of the temperature, but she barely needs it – she can pretty much do this by feel. When the temperature reaches 130 degrees, she holds the open valve under the running water until the AV, made of translucent amber latex, plumps up like a Ball Park Frank. She rolls up her sleeve to stick her bare arm inside to test the snugness. Western Hanover, who's twelve years old, doesn't like the same tight fit that the younger stallions go for, so Kaufman opens the valve and lets the water run out until it feels just right.

Outside, Western Hanover is pacing by the stimulation mare. He's so worked up about his afternoon chores that he's starting to lather at the shoulders. The stimulation or tease mare stands in the stocks, a horse-size enclosure of steel pipes built high enough to keep her from kicking the stallion and low enough to leave her rump exposed to his investigations. The tease mare is a regular Standardbred mare in natural heat and scheduled for artificial insemination later in the day. This brief encounter is the closest she'll ever get to a real live stud.

Western Hanover, despite his excitement, makes no attempt to crash over the steel pipes and take the mare where she stands. Instead, he tugs at the lead shank and turns away, trying to run the tight half-circle back to the phantom mount, a padded pommel horse about four feet tall. He strains to get to it, with such wildness and urgency that Bip Chronister, the penis washer, slaps him across the face with a wet towel to remind him of his manners. Kaufman, who's been waiting at the door between the prep room and the breeding shed, checking the progress of his excitement through a window in the door, quickly enters the shed. In the lab, you can see Kaufman, who's tall and willowy and just a year out of veterinary school, still shedding some of the whiz-kid habits – watching, asking questions, comparing notes. But once she opens the door to the breeding shed, she's all business. The stallion handler, responding to her entrance, immediately lets the horse take over the choreography, and he circles to the phantom and mounts without any of the halfheartedness you see in those who feel they have to settle for second best. As he comes down on the phantom, Kaufman deftly snags his penis one-handed and diverts the flailing erection into the AV. She presses the whole Missouri-style contraption as close to the padded mount as possible and Western Hanover quickly delivers about 30 cc's of Standardbred genes in the usual medium; Kaufman pulls the AV away. She tilts it so the liquid runs down to the bottom of the disposable collection liner – a sort of generously proportioned lubricated condom, called a Whirl-Pak, that fits inside the AV – and since Hanover uses the open-ended Missouri model, all those in the room can see for themselves that Western Hanover has done a good day's work: one sample of posterity to be divided six ways, at twenty thousand per, for a $120,000 worth of work.

'Isn't he a good boy?' Kaufman says, in the tender singsong tones some people use to address an adorable dog.

Back in the lab, Neil Hanchett prepares the sample. He puts a drop of the semen on a glass plate and slides it under a microscope so the SpermaCue can take a census, and Neil can calculate how many times he can safely divide the total population – Dr J won't send out fewer than a billion in a shipment. A TV monitor hooked up to the SpermaCue displays the hordes of sperm, live and in black and white. A gang of them have latched on to something ('I think that's a piece of smegma,' Dr J says), which they're pushing mightily across the screen. Most of the sperm seem to know where they're going, but a few wander aimlessly in a circle, like crazies who should never have been let out on work-release. Dr J watches the screen – too many crazies for her. 'The quality gets a lot better as you get into the spring,' she says.

The Panderosa, a son of Western Hanover, is up next. 'He's a bit of a goof,' Dr J says, as the five-year-old bay begins checking out the tease mare. It's only his second season at stud, and he still dawdles a bit, mostly because of lack of concentration; the stallion handler has to rattle his lead shank to make him pay attention. 'Western, he's as automatic as you see a horse,' Dr J says. 'Most of the others have their good days and bad days.' But after a few rattles and a nibble or two near the mare's tail, The Panderosa starts to focus and he, too, turns under minimal guidance and circles quickly to the phantom. He's almost a full hand taller than his father, so his assault on the mount looks and sounds more brutal. Dr J, who barely makes it up to his haunches to begin with, ducks under his approach and deftly contains his excitement in the opening of the disposable liner. As she leans into him, she keeps one hand on the Missouri model and the other at the base of his urethra, feeling for the pulsations that signal the end of his exertions. It isn't long.

'You're a freakin' nut, you know that?' Dr J tells The Panderosa. He hasn't really been that nutty – more like scary and single-minded. Her gruff, shouted endearment comes off as sisterly.

As she pulls the AV away, The Panderosa goes all limp and rubbery and nearly falls off the phantom as he attempts his dismount. Everybody holds his or her breath, but after a quick stumble and a nimble recovery from this Honcho-like semiblackout, The Pande-rosa lifts up his head and looks back at the mare, in flustered recognition. The suddenness of it all makes people laugh, both out of relief and out of pleasure in his dunderheaded charm – it's just the sort of crazy, clumsy move that only a real athlete could pull off.

The vets get into a rhythm after that, working separately, one prepping an AV while another collects. Lindy Lane comes in and goes right to work and, sure enough, as he rears up onto the phantom, he squeals like a pig. Back in the lab, his sample on the monitor looks like Grand Central Station, crowded and full of purpose. This pleases Dr J. 'See that sperm? That's about as good as you get.' Her happiness is short-lived: Dragon Again, standing his first season at stud, is collected next, and his sperm run around in circles, wild and unfocused, like a pee wee soccer team on an outing to Chuck E. Cheese.

Kevin Conley

The last two stallions go to Jacqueline O'Donnell, a rangy news-anchor blond in big Cosby-style sweaters. Both stallions, Arturo and Sierra Kosmos, fall into the special-request category. Arturo, a durable, hard-running horse who raced thirty-one times as a three-year-old, is a position freak. Unlike the other stallions, who find enough titillation in the warmth and individual fit of their personal AVs, Arturo likes a little extra torque. To accommodate his wishes, O'Donnell has to make sure she positions his AV under his body, instead of off to the side of the mount, the way all the other stallions take it. With this arrangement, Arturo can come down hard and squeeze his own erection (and practically burst his AV) on the back edge of the pommel horse.

'You'd think he would hurt himself,' the stallion handler, Evelyn Roberts says, watching and wincing from across the shed.

There's none of this obsessive-compulsive frenzy about Sierra Kosmos. When he arrives, the pace of action slackens and the movement of the people slows. With the younger, hot-blooded stallions, the crew has to react quickly, giving ground and responding alertly to their whims. But with Sierra Kosmos standing flatfooted by the tease mare, everyone just hangs around staring at his penis. O'Donnell keeps popping to the observation window to check for signs of interest. Bip, the penis washer, a man with big hands and a well-padded body that could probably absorb a kick or two, shakes his head, until finally Sierra Kosmos works up something he can sling around.

'He's dripping, now,' Bip calls, alerting O'Donnell to the appearance of precoital fluid. O'Donnell rushes out. As Sierra Kosmos rears, the vet not only corrals him into his AV but also places a hot towel by his balls – a little added stimulation to help keep his mind on the task at hand.

'There you go,' O'Donnell says, at once tender and businesslike, like a nurse giving a sponge bath. 'Good boy.'

Back in the prep room, the FedEx and courier boxes are starting to pile up. Another stack of packages sits by the sliding window, for local pickups. The boxes are improbably light, most of their bulk devoted to Styrofoam insulation, into which two tubes of fully extended semen fit snugly beside a cold pack. As Dr J loads about twenty or so boxes into her SUV to take back to the office, I ask her what she tells civilians about her job in the breeding shed. 'They can't grasp it until they see it. They don't understand,' she says, shrugging defensively. 'And then when they see it, it all makes sense.' She talks instead about the shape of the year on a horse farm: foaling and palpating mares and collecting stallions in the spring; prepping the yearlings for the sales in the summer; then going to the sales in the fall. 'And then December and January come along, and there's nothing to do. I think I get clinically depressed.'

ELEVEN

Popes in the Breeding Shed

T HERE ARE LOTS OF family farms in the bluegrass. Take the Taylor family, the four sons of the former Gainesway farm manager Joe Taylor, who run Taylor Made Farm, a commercial breeding operation that opened in 1976 and now does about $60 million worth of business every year at Keeneland alone. Taylor Made is a family farm in the way that Ford Motor Company is a family business. Then there's the Hancock family, which runs Claiborne, a three-thousand-acre Bourbon County farm that's been churning out champions and hall-of-fame horses since 1910. Claiborne is a family farm in the way that Windsor Castle is a home.

The McLeans, of Crestwood Farm, a seven-hundred-acre place on the northwest edge of Lexington, are not in their league at all. Grandison is the youngest; she helps manage the office. Marc is the farm manager; his older brother, Pope Junior, handles the financial side. The father, Pope Senior, started it all, forty years ago, and he seems most at home talking to clients in the breeding shed. The McLeans keep the Crestwood operation pretty simple — a lot of the interdepartmental communications seem to take place by Post-its and torn envelopes taped to the door.

Still, the McLeans have seen a lot of wealthy neighbors come and go. Both Ivan Boesky and Leona Helmsley lived next door for a while, the former at Blackburn Correctional Complex and the latter at the Federal Medical Center, two of the facilities at the redbrick summer camp of a federal penitentiary complex just beyond the stallion paddocks. The neighbors to the west, over the hills and past the broodmares, tend to stick around a bit longer than the inmates, but not much. First there was Tom Collins, who named his place On the Rocks Farm; the name proved to be more prophetic than funny, and he left after five years. Then came Franklin Groves (a person, not a subdivision) who called it North Ridge Farm, and tried to turn it into a showcase; he stayed from 1984 to 1991. The present owner, who calls the place Vinery, is Dr Tom Simon; he seems to be a doctor of corporate takeovers. He's been around for a couple of years.

True to his name, Groves planted thousands of trees. Simon specializes in building fences. The McLeans, who are all modest and polite, would never say a word against their bigger-budget neighbors, but that doesn't stop them from being amused by all the activity. 'One day, we looked up and there must have been fifteen bulldozers lined up on this side of the road over on the hill there,' Pope Senior says. 'They were all aimed this way, as if they were coming at us to push us off the face of the earth.'

'A lot of the farms that come in here get a little top-heavy and load all these expenses on,' says Pope Junior, who did a stint as a broker for Dean Witter before he came back home to work on the family farm. 'Then all of a sudden they've got to start making their operation pay for it.'

Pope Senior guides the conversation away from the hint of censure and back toward gentle anecdote. It seems that a friend who wanted to get into the horse business was converting some tobacco barns into stables. 'I told him, "Well, the most important thing is to be sure they have slate roofs." And about six months later, I bumped into him and he said, "I thought you were serious about that." ' It's an easy mistake to make. Pope Senior is tall, slim, silver-haired, and literally upright. No pillar of the community looks more

They talk easily about the intricacies of the business. But they're not so comfortable talking about their success. When I ask a few questions about Crestwood's solid record and how grateful their partners must feel about it, Pope Junior says, 'Well, it's a risky business and – We've been able to at least protect people and maybe – I think we've done pretty well.'

The father interrupts, and is even more eloquently unpromotional: 'They seem to keep coming back, so . . . So, we're doing something, I guess.'

Given such reticence, the bragging duties must fall to others, and Jim Smith, an old friend of Pope Senior's and Crestwood's veterinarian from the very beginning, is glad to oblige. Smith, who counts Coolmore among his list of clients, points out the biggest recommendation of the McLeans' family farm: horses are their only income.

Pope Senior agrees. 'There are some that come into the business – well, just like North Ridge.' He's referring to Franklin Groves, who'd made his pile building huge public projects, like the Bonneville Dam on the Columbia River between Washington and Oregon, then spent it turning his horse farm into a showcase. 'He was coming in as a hobby. Of course, he obviously *wanted* to make money at it, but we *have* to. We don't have some other source that we're clipping coupons from.'

Pope McLean's father was a doctor, and he wasn't all that interested in horses, which, in Lexington, means he only had twenty-five acres out on Newtown Pike, where he kept just one mare, a Thoroughbred that he'd been given half an interest in. In 1956, that mare, Wicki Wicki, was bred to Oil Capital, and Pope raised the foal, Oil Wick, a gray colt who soon became a gelding. When Oil Wick won the Kentucky Jockey Club Stakes, at Churchill Downs, in 1959, Pope switched majors from premed to agriculture, which is not an act of rebellion in the bluegrass. Dr McLean gave him a piece of his share in Oil Wick, and Pope has been making money in the business ever since.

His progress can be charted by leaps of real estate. For five years, he worked mostly alone on his father's twenty-five acres, raising a yearling or two for the fall sales. In 1965, he leased a hundred-acre section of Poplar Hill Farm, on Russell Cave Road, and in 1970, he moved to a four-hundred-acre place that he leased for five years until he could buy it outright – with an additional hundred acres – in 1975. He added the final two hundred and fifteen acres in 1998, to bring the spread to its current seven hundred and fifteen acres. But as Crestwood Farm grew, McLean stuck to the same inch-by-inch philosophy: get the best mares you can afford; catch a quality stud early in his career when he's cheap; then take the profits from the yearling sales to buy better mares.

Of course, everybody wants to catch a quality stud when he's cheap, but McLean has actually pulled the trick off. He bred eight mares to Storm Cat when everybody was giving up on him and his stud fee was at its lowest point, $20,000. One of the foals turned out to be Sardula, who won the Kentucky Oaks in 1994.

What he doesn't try to do is breed something to catch the eye of the Coolmore crowd or the Maktoums, because to do so, he'd have to tie up all his available capital in stud fees. Instead, he puts out good-value athletes for the sporting crowd. The Crestwood motto, 'We raise runners,' may sound stunningly obvious, like a car dealer saying 'We sell vehicles.' But buyers recognize what the motto leaves unsaid: 'And we don't raise ten-million-dollar yearlings who never make it to the starting gate.'

In 1993, the McLeans decided to expand their business and stand a few stallions. The stallion business requires complicated financial agreements, but the basic model is the syndicate. The syndicate arrangement recognizes that stallions are too risky and too expensive to own outright, so ownership is divided, typically, into forty shares, which the breeding farm sells. Breeders can buy one or more shares, and each one entitles the shareholder to an ownership interest and a lifetime breeding right, which means that every year he or she can either breed one mare to the stallion or sell that year's breeding to the highest bidder. (Recent shareholder agreements have recognized the increases in stallions' productivity, and a single share often allows the breeder to breed two mares a year to the stallion.) Of course, like all business arrangements, there are infinite variations on this basic deal.

When a breeding farm gets the right to stand a stallion, it agrees to handle the syndication and arrange for and carry out the breedings. In exchange for discharging these duties, the farm is usually given five breeding rights or 'farm shares'. Of course, there are simpler ways to do it. You could buy a cheap horse outright. Or you could lease him. When the McLeans decided to get into stallions, they didn't set up any multimillion-dollar syndications. They stuck to their budget, and looked for a bargain horse.

The first stallion they got was Discover, a Claiborne Farm homebred who retired with $700,000 in winnings. Landing Discover was a coup, not because the horse was all that famous, even to the guys who hang out at OTB. Landing Discover was a coup because he was Seth Hancock's horse. Hancock's the fourth generation of Hancocks – the line runs back to a captain in the Confederacy – to run Claiborne, whose sires have produced fourteen Kentucky Derby winners and five Triple Crown winners. And while it's wrong to think that Kentucky breeding is controlled by an old-boys network (it's actually very democratic, in the way that high-stakes poker is democratic), still there are a lot of old boys around, playing golf at the Idle Hour Country Club and going to Kentucky basketball games together. So when Seth Hancock deals one of his good horses to a stallion start-up – well, the word gets around.

The second horse that Crestwood landed was Storm Boot, a mean and deceptively fast chestnut colt from Storm Cat's first crop. He's a pure sprinter, short, bulky, nearly bandy-legged with muscle. He has Mike Tyson's build, and his temperament, too, and he has the bad habit of picking up grooms by his teeth – grabbing them by the leg or the pectoral muscle – then dropping them somewhere else more to his liking. But this ornery son of Storm Cat went to stud at just the right time. In the middle of his first breeding season, the Storm Cat filly Sardula won the Kentucky Oaks, and Tabasco Cat won the Preakness and the Belmont. Storm Cat's stud fee headed toward six figures. To book to Storm Boot, it cost you only a thousand.

They certainly weren't picky over mares that first year. 'They'd look good enough on paper,' McLean says. 'And then they'd show up at the breeding shed –' He shakes his head, recalling Storm Boot's sad parade of sickly, lame, and aged partners.

But Storm Boot managed to get runners out of that herd of hopeless nags. One mare, Assagai's Ex, had had seven foals, not one of whom had ever made it to the racetrack, let alone the winner's circle, but her Storm Boot colt won a $100,000 graded-stakes race. It seems Storm Boot had a genetic assertiveness to match his distemper – good news for the newcomer and his new home. In the next few years, demand grew and his stud fee leapfrogged, from $2,000 to $6,000 to $10,000. By the time I visited, he was up to $15,000 – moderate for Kentucky, astronomical in any other state.

Crestwood's success with Storm Boot has attracted other stallion owners, and now the McLeans have a tidy little list, full of the sort of studs that Pope McLean has always preferred: leading-sire look-alikes and big-bang-for-your-buck horses, with a stud fee that costs less than your car. For $7,500, you can book to Petionville, a son of the leading sire Seeking the Gold, who stands at Claiborne for $250,000. For $6,000, you can get Dixieland Heat, son of the

$75,000 stallion Dixieland Band. You'll be hoping he'll give you something like Xtra Heat, a knockaround bay filly with an upside-down question mark on her forehead. Xtra Heat passed through the auction block three times – selling for $9,100; $4,700; and $5,000, in one sale after the other; then she went to the track and won seventeen of twenty races, earning over a million dollars, more than a hundred times her daddy's stud fee. There are a lot of buyers at Keeneland, Fasig-Tipton, and the Ocala Breeders' Sales Company who never put down a bid on Xtra Heat. Now they study her win pictures and wonder, *What was I thinking?*

The teaser stallion on duty at the Crestwood breeding shed is a squat fellow, meaty, powerful, and benign. He's a crossbreed, the foal of a nurse mare and a Thoroughbred, and he gets his peaceable temperament from his draft horse side. His name, Picho, is scrawled in chalk on a tablet-sized blackboard beside his stall, because teasers don't get the engraved brass nameplates that the stallions do and because teaser duty rotates. They used to call him Pito, which means 'penis' in Spanish, or actually 'wingding' or 'weewee' or whatever nursery euphemism you prefer. The name led to an encounter with a lady vet, apparently a non–Spanish speaker, who saw 'Pito' on his blackboard and said, famously, 'Oh, Pito. I love Pito! That's my favorite!'

Picho is good at his job, uncomplaining and unfailingly eager, and – an added benefit for the men who muck out his stall – he has unusual self-discipline: he's stall-broken and, according to the stallion manager, Rogelio Castillo, will wait patiently until he's let outdoors to seek relief. As Castillo tells me this, I peer into his stall and, sure enough, Picho stands in the middle of his unsoiled straw, heartbreakingly still.

Right across from Picho's stall, the prep work for the afternoon breeding session begins quietly. It's April now, almost exactly halfway through the breeding season, and people file in and start setting up, one by one. Marc McLean comes in through the big barn door, slides it closed behind him – this is the coldest day of the April cold snap – and walks to a hook on the far wall, where he hangs a clipboard with the afternoon's slate of mares. Rob Keck, who preps the mares during the sessions, comes out of the lab room and lines up tail wraps on a wooden ledge. Back down the hall, where the stallions are stabled, Pope Junior talks with an owner. When his father arrives to take over the chatting, Pope Junior goes into a stall to clip a shank on the leadoff stallion.

The stallion barn is long and dark, with stained wood, thick beams, and low ceilings to accommodate the hay stored on the floor above. The breeding shed, at the end of the row of dark stalls, is a bright contrast, painted white, sunny, and lined with overhead windows, airy and double-tall. It's an old barn that's been on the property since at least the thirties, when Thomas Piatt, the first head of the Keeneland Association, used it for his stallions, and when the barn door opens for the first ready mare of the afternoon, the view of horse country is practically unchanged from Piatt's heyday. Even the prison over the hills keeps horses. About seventy Thoroughbreds have been sent to the penitentiary stables as a twofold act of mercy: prisoners pick up employable skills, such as grooming and farriery, and racetrack also-rans are spared a trip to the slaughterhouse.

With the arrival of the first mare, Explosive Start, it's as if the music starts and the dance begins. The owner hands her over to Keck and retreats to the sidelines. 'I want a filly this time,' the owner tells Pope Senior, who stands beside him.

Pope Junior appears with the stallion she's here for, Dusty Screen, and says, 'Just as long as we get you one or the other.'

Pope Senior says, 'These vets can go in at about a hundred and fifty days now and tell you whether it's going to be a colt or a filly.

And they're right about 50 per cent of the time.' This typically dry remark goes over the head of the owner, or maybe he's too busy spectating to hear it. The man talks instead about the price of a halter and the cocktail of hormones that he's given his mare – Regumate, prostaglandin – to get her ready for her date. Nervous chatter, by the pace of it.

Dusty Screen steps into the shed under Pope Junior's lead. Catching the owner appraising the stud, he says, 'He's a good racehorse.'

'Yeah, I know,' the mare's owner says. 'I bet on that horse right there.'

The mare parts her legs and empties her bladder onto the wood-chip floor in a long-lasting stream – just another trick of seduction in a mare's arsenal of feminine wiles. Rob Keck, who is standing closest to the display, sees me taking notes, and says 'Real glamorous, huh?' then breaks into spontaneous oration: 'The pageantry! The glamour of the Thoroughbred!'

But Dusty Screen – he totally goes for it. He can barely wait long enough for Pope Senior to snag the shower nozzle and rinse him off. He rears, he mounts – and she changes her mind and tries to skedaddle. The stud backs off, a little flummoxed, but now the men on the ground get serious, as if they take this personally; for the second jump, the twitch gets tightened and Pope Junior and Castillo hang on to Dusty Screen's front legs, anchoring him to the mare, inching him forward to the final goal, tug-of-war style.

Marc McLean is concentrating, his hand right there in the middle of the act. But he reserves such seriousness for the clashes of horseflesh. Between breedings, he chats comfortably with the owners and handlers who drive the mares to the farm, and he tells me the poignant story of Skitchy, one of the Crestwood teasers. It seems that Skitchy was doing a test jump on a mare and, just as he was rearing up, the mare kicked. Unfortunately for the teaser, her timing was perfect. Her hoof landed right on his penis and split it in two. The vet had no choice. He had to amputate, turning Skitchy into a strange surgical variant of the gelding: an intact horse with no penis. All of the drive. None of the wherewithal.

'He pees both ways now,' Marc says. 'He still teases, though. He's still got a good libido.'

Marc is a boyish thirty-three, with pale blue eyes and dark, Dennis-the-Menace hair. His brother, Pope, is a couple inches taller, a couple years older, and with a slight curl of the lip that marks him as the 'dangerous' brother, in the sense that Ricky was the dangerous Nelson. The two of them are far from identical, but the differences are hard to untangle from the similarities – if you meet them together, you tend to talk about them together, the way you might say 'the twin with short hair' or 'the quiet Beatle'.

All the McLeans are remarkably considerate with one another, behaving with an easy collegiality, and, incredible as it sounds, with no evidence of the preserved-in-amber arguments that lurk in most family scenarios. In short, they act like grown-ups. There's a photograph in an old *Blood-Horse* of Pope McLean, Sr., at Keeneland, in his standard outfit of chinos, button-down, and elbow-patch sweater, watching a pair of buyers assess one of his horses. He stands at the edge of the picture, hands in his pockets, about fifteen feet away from the buyers; the caption says, 'I hate to bother buyers . . . but like to be available.' That seems to be his philosophy with his sons, too.

The next mare in the door is Meadowfold, from Upson Downs. She's here for Storm Boot, who, Marc tells me, has such a point-and-shoot libido that they wait till the last second to bring him into the shed. Meadowfold's a maiden, a balky type not to be trusted around the farm's top stud, so they call on Picho to take a jump or two. He comes out of his stall, low-slung and aproned, and when he gets near the mare he lets loose a rumble in the sexy basso range, like one of those candlelight-and-Champale singers, Barry White or Teddy Pendergrass. It goes on for a while ('hmmmmm . . . hmm-m-m-m-m-m-m-m'), full of tenderness and longing and such sheer volume that the shed can barely hold the sound. When Castillo yanks him down, Picho just turns and walks back to his stall, and the mare looks ready.

Storm Boot is led in right away. He's a chestnut – liver chestnut, actually, a dark-chocolate variation of the shade – and he's short, generously listed at 15.3 hands high: Thoroughbreds normally range from 15 to 17 hands, but the official height is often exaggerated, due to breeders' preference for tall horses. As he walks out of the dark hall into the breeding shed toward the mare, I'm surprised at how easy it is to look over him to watch the Popes, both father and son, calmly eyeing his arousal.

But height isn't everything. When Storm Boot rears up and the massive bulwark of his shoulders lands on the back of the mare, he's suddenly towering and forceful. He bellows, shattering the moody ambience left over from Picho's little hey-baby moment, and the maiden mare is startled back to reality. She tries to kick, and when that doesn't work because her front leg is hobbled, she starts to squirm away.

'Come on, Mom,' Pope Senior says.

When Storm Boot comes back to earth for a moment, he paws at the ground in front of him like a bull. Even in a job that calls for aggression, he's unusually aggressive. Most stallions simply rear and land on a mare, using their front legs for balance, and all the muscular exertion takes place in their hindquarters. But Storm Boot wrestles the mare with his forequarters, his shoulders clamping down, his front legs pulling at her body and almost scampering in the air around her as he heaves himself forward. The mare owner can see what he's paying for: muscle, muscle, and more muscle.

Compared to Storm Boot in rut, Arnold Schwarzenegger looks like a rag doll.

When it's over, the owner seems relieved, even a little forlorn. 'Once it got started, she was all right,' he says, and leads his mare back to the van.

TWELVE

Horse Sex: The Conservative View

P OPE MᴄLᴇᴀɴ'ꜱ Crestwood Farm has eight houses on
seven hundred acres. Seth Hancock's Claiborne Farm has
twenty-five houses scattered over the farm's three thousand acres,
with another fourteen houses in nearby Paris, Kentucky. Both
places are family farms, but many more families – from the farm
manager, Gus Koch, and his wife and ten children, to the stallion
manager, Jim Zajic; the farm vet; the stallion grooms; the broodmare division; the yearling managers; even the local football coach –
live at Claiborne and depend on its successful tradition and continuing success.

Claiborne's tradition has its roots in the nineteenth century – in
1864, Captain Richard Hancock, of the Army of Northern
Virginia, married Thomasina Harris, the daughter of a Virginia
horseman who owned Ellerslie Farm, outside Charlottesburg. In
1908, the Captain's son Arthur Boyd Hancock married a Kentucky horsewoman, Nancy Tucker Clay. When she inherited a
farm in Bourbon County in 1910, Hancock named the place
Claiborne after her and transferred the bulk of the family's
breeding operations from Ellerslie, in Virginia, to Claiborne, in
Kentucky. His son, A. B. (Bull) Hancock, Jr., took over the place
in 1952, and at Bull's death in 1972, Bull's son Seth became
Claiborne's president.

After nearly thirty years at the helm, Seth Hancock has the

careworn look of the naturally modest man in charge of a complex operation. Though he has successfully steered the business since the days of Secretariat, it hasn't always been easy. Just months after his father died on September 12, 1972, the estate executors, acting on the advice of the farm advisers (longtime clients Ogden Phipps, Charles Kenney, and William Haggin Perry) passed over his older, maverick brother, Arthur III, in favor of the younger, more serious son. By early February 1973, Seth Hancock was busy syndicating Secretariat (who had yet to win any of his Triple Crown races), for $5 million, more than anyone had ever paid for a horse. And Hancock had to make it up as he went along.

'See, my father died when I was twenty-three years old,' Hancock explains. 'And I went to prep school from the time I was fourteen to eighteen, and college from the time I was eighteen to twenty-one, and unfortunately, I never really had much tutoring by him. I guess the most things that I learned from him were right after he died, going back and looking at his recent work. And trying to look at a mare, and knowing what she'd been on the racetrack and what she was back here at the farm and then seeing how he'd matched her up. But I never heard him say, "Well, I bred Moccasin to Round Table because of *this*." But I went back and I thought, *Well, is it because Moccasin is a big old rawboned mare and Round Table's kind of a small type of horse?* So I just tried to read his mind. But I never got to hear him *speak* his mind about those things.'

There is a theory that horses defer to humans because our ears are naturally pinned back against our heads, the way a horse's get when he's angry or set on having his way. According to this theory, a horse takes one look at the willful little creature with the dangerous ears and decides to give in, at least until we're in a better, more reasonable mood.

To a horse, Seth Hancock looks like a man in a reasonable mood. His ears are big, like Prince Charles's, and they stick out just enough to put a Thoroughbred at ease. Perhaps the horses pick up on other cues, too. Hancock is lean and soft-spoken. When he comes by the breeding shed, as he will if it's an important mating – when, say, his home-bred mare Preach, dam of Pulpit, is going to his promising sophomore stallion Arch – Hancock stands patiently, with his hips swayed loosely forward, like a man watching his tee shot. He doesn't litter the air with small talk, but when he's approached his brief responses sound like the final word.

The breeding shed at Claiborne is the fastest I've been to, and much of that speed can be attributed to Hancock's conservative management of the stallions: he likes his stallions to have a light workload, a high libido, and a realistic stud fee. Back in his spacious and book-lined office after the breeding session, he explains why: 'This is kind of a crude analogy,' he tells me. 'But if I have an ejaculate of semen that's thirty cc's and you have an ejaculate of semen that's five cc's, which ejaculate has the best chance of containing a sperm cell that is the absolute Michael Jordan of all sperm cells? Mine that's got thirty or yours that's got five? Which one?'

I admit that his sperm has the better chance.

'I've got better chances, right? Now, the scientist will say, "Well, that's ridiculous. It doesn't take but one sperm cell, and it makes no difference how weak or how strong he might be, to get the mare in foal." And he's right. The weakest sperm cell of the bunch, he can swim up there. He can fertilize the egg. The mare can get in foal. She can have the foal. But what if I've got this Michael Jordan sperm cell and you've got this little weak one? Well, when my foal comes out, I might have a great, big, strong athletic foal. You might have a foal, yes, but he may be a little bitty of a runty that couldn't outrun me or you. I mean, maybe that's an oversimplification. But it's truly the way I view it. And I know – *I know for sure* – that if I'm breeding my horse three times every *two* days, and you're breeding your horse three times *every* day, I'm gonna have thirty cc's and y'all are gonna have five. Now, the other part of my little equation there might be wrong. But I know that my ejaculate is going to have more volume than yours. There ain't no doubt about that.'

The first thing you see as you open the side door of the Claiborne office and head toward the stallion barns is the graveyard of leading sires, a grassy ell ringed with bushes and studded with mossy headstones dating back more than seventy years. 'There are twenty-one horses buried here, but there's only five that are buried in their entire body.' Joe Peel tells me. He's been at Claiborne for fifteen years, moving from yearlings to stallions to his current position as the twitch man in the breeding shed, and he knows this stuff cold. 'The older tradition of burying Thoroughbreds was with the head, the hooves, and the heart – the three main ingredients to making a great racehorse.'

There's another, even older tradition of throwing in the testicles, too – that final ingredient that turns a champion into the total package. But no one at Claiborne admits to it.

'There's two Triple Crown winners buried here. One of them is buried whole, Secretariat.' Peel grew up in Bourbon County, on his grandparents' dairy farm – a hard living, he says, that made him like to work. Peel has a friendly squint, a Dale Earnhardt mustache, a farm twang, and a catchy show-and-tell enthusiasm for his job and surroundings. He rattles off the histories of the four other horses buried entire: Swale, Claiborne's first Kentucky Derby winner; Round Table, the leading money earner of the fifties; Mr Prospector, the leading sire of the past twenty years; and Nijinsky, the English Triple Crown winner and son of Northern Dancer. (In October 2001, following my visit, a sixth horse,

Unbridled, was buried whole, at another Thoroughbred graveyard on the farm, after he colicked in the aftermath of two colon surgeries and had to be euthanized.) Then Peel paces me through the ones reduced to their prized bits, a list of stallions that shaped the breed for the past century.

There's Bold Ruler, the father of Secretariat and the most successful sire since Lexington, the leading sire of the nineteenth century; Nasrullah, a British champion that Bull Hancock bought in 1949, with Harry Guggenheim and William Woodward, for $340,000; Princequillo, an Irish colt, who, according to Peel, shipped to this country in 1940 in a submarine; Blenheim II, another key stallion import, bought by Bull's father, Arthur Boyd Hancock, Sr., in 1936 for $250,000; Sir Gallahad III, a French horse that A. B. Hancock bought, the foundation sire for the renewal of an inbred American bloodstock; Gallant Fox, from Sir Gallahad III's first American crop, the Triple Crown winner in 1930, and the only one to sire another Triple Crown winner, Omaha, who won in 1935.

Only one of the horses mentioned above, Swale, a Seattle Slew colt, raced in the yellow silks of Claiborne; he won the Kentucky Derby and the Belmont in 1984, then, eight days after the latter victory, died of a heart attack. As Richard J. Hancock, the Confederate captain who launched the family's breeding operations in 1877, realized early on, the safest bet in the Thoroughbred business lies not in breeding the occasional champion for yourself – the dream of the sportsman – but in controlling the bloodlines they come from. From the arrival of Sir Gallahad III in 1926 to the death of Mr Prospector in 1999, a span of seventy-three years, Claiborne stood the country's leading sire twenty-seven times.

Peel walks over to the yellow-and-white stallion barns to introduce me to the current sires, resting in their stalls after their morning's exertions. He brings out one after the other: the leading sire Seeking the Gold ('This stallion is one of them aggressive stallions at times'), the excitable Pulpit ('He just bred this morning, but still, you know, he's ready'), the wonderfully named Horse Chestnut, who's a chestnut horse. It's a good thing that the Claiborne stallions don't read, because the list of former tenants on the stall doors, champions and leading sires whose brass name-plates have never been removed, could easily induce performance anxiety in a more literary sort of stallion. Horse Chestnut's name-plate, for example, sits under Mr Prospector's; Pulpit's under Round Table's. Poor Unbridled (still hale and showing off for visitors at the time of my visit) has to contend with the legacy of Bold Ruler and Secretariat.

However, none of them seem to suffer the slightest anxiety in that regard. Studs being studs, they tend to display the opposite syndrome. Horse Chestnut, for example, comes out of his stall in a state of semi-excitement, a condition that reveals a black band near the end of his penis.

'The ring is on to keep this horse from ejaculating,' Peel explains. The band cuts off the blood flow when the penis achieves a certain size. 'He'll be daydreaming in the stall there, and, you know, they get theirself worked up to where they can actually ejaculate. So that keeps him from doing that. We had to put that ring on, I believe it's been on about three weeks. When he'd go down to breed the mare, his libido wasn't sound enough. He wasn't acting like he wanted to breed, he wasn't covering the mares good, so this keeps him intact.'

Peel tells me about an earlier device ('the olden way') that accomplished the same thing: a girth strap with a steel-wool-like brush placed where it would discourage any solitary whacking. Then he brings out the farm's senior stallion, Danzig, the country's leading sire three years running in the early nineties. He's twenty-four now, with a slab fracture in his left front knee – there's literally a slab underneath his skin, as if he were shoplifting a paperback. Danzig's blind on his left side, from fresh creosote that got in his eye twelve years ago when they were repainting the place for Queen Elizabeth's visit, and he's used sparingly in the breeding shed these days. When he does breed, though, he brings in over a quarter of a million dollars a shot.

It takes great restraint to pass up the sort of income that Danzig can bring in, and perhaps only a place like Claiborne could do it. The farm has benefitted from its long-term associations – especially with the Phipps family, New York racing bluebloods whose mares, among the most coveted in the world, have boarded at Claiborne for more than seventy years. The combination of Claiborne stallions and Phipps mares creates the sort of virtuous circle that breeders pray to be part of: boarder mares, like the Phippses', get first crack at the stallions, and those superior mares foal stakes-winning horses that burnish the reputation of their sires. In the next generation, the best stakes-winning horses retire to Claiborne, for the chance to breed to mares like the Phippses'. It's the bloodstock version of the rich getting richer, and it relies not on an old-boys network but on an old-mares network.

Claiborne can afford to rest Danzig and limit his book of mares because the system runs, to a great degree, on scarcity. For example, whenever the Phippses cull their herd of broodmares and sell off the poorer individuals, the prices they get are always among the highest, even though everyone knows they're selling inferior stock, precisely because the Phipps bloodlines so rarely come to the market.

Hancock offers another example. Six or eight years ago, he says, the Coolmore stallion Woodman and the Claiborne stallion Seeking the Gold were equally sought after. 'If you asked a person which one of these stallions you like the best, Woodman or Seeking the Gold, there'd've been seven of them would have said Seeking the Gold. Five of them might have said Woodman. So they were basically six of one, half-dozen of the other. Man, you go out and ask anybody today and they'd laugh at you. They'd say, "Are you kidding me? Seeking the Gold is four times as sireworthy as Woodman is." Now why is that? If they were equal six or eight years ago, or close to being equal, why is one of them so far superior to the other today? Is it because Woodman was bred to three hundred mares a year, and Seeking the Gold was only bred to ninety? I don't know. But that's a fact. You don't have to take my word for it. Go see what their stud fees were in 1995 and see what they are now. You can get a season of Woodman now for twenty-five thousand dollars. It'd cost you two hundred and fifty thousand to breed to Seeking the Gold – if you could get to him.'

I visited Ashford Stud, Coolmore's Kentucky farm, back in January, weeks after Woodman had gotten back from his shuttle-stallion duties down in Australia, and just days after he'd gotten out of the quarantine mandated for horses returning from abroad. It was the middle of Keeneland's January breeding-stock sale, and Ashford Stud was throwing an open house in hopes of luring in breeders to check out their stallions.

Ashford Stud and Claiborne Farm aren't just different in philosophy; they look like two different worlds. Claiborne is undeniably beautiful, but with an unfussy beauty of rolling hills, huge forty-acre fields, graceful old trees, converted tobacco barns. Across from the stallion paddocks, there's a scattering of modest houses for the farm personnel, single-story dwellings with aluminum siding. 'We have some good horses here,' Gus Koch says, 'but we're a working farm.' Ashford, on the other hand, looks like a lordly estate, with stone walls and a colonnade of trees lining the long drive to the manor house that serves as an office. The barns have slate roofs and sky-blue doors and spires like the ones at Churchill Downs, and when you go inside the stables, the sun streams in through the dark bars on the windows and everywhere you turn, you hear the gentle horse-manlike murmur of Irish accents. Even the black guys speak with a brogue.

Aisling Cross, the Ashford pedigree consultant and resident glamour gal, led a group of us gawkers through this living picture book of race history. They kept bringing out stallions to show off. I saw Fusaichi Pegasus, the 2000 Kentucky Derby winner, who'd just had his first test breeding that morning – he actually capered when he was led out into the sun. I saw the 1995 Kentucky Derby winner Thunder Gulch, who stood patiently while a visitor posed beside him for a snapshot.

The stallion roster made for lovely sightseeing, but Woodman was the only one I really wanted to see. Like Storm Cat, Wood-man represents an extreme of the stud's profession. Storm Cat commands the top fee, but Woodman actually spends the most time on the job, and I had the feeling that many men, setting aside moral considerations and allowing for certain superficial differences between species, would rather trade places with Woodman than with Storm Cat. I wanted to see if he looked happy.

It took a while for them to bring him out, because, unlike the other stallions, who were idling in the stables, waiting for their frequent star turns during the open house, Woodman was off alone in the fields. Aisling Cross apologized for the delay, but, really, she had other things on her mind. She'd just gotten engaged and people were asking her what kind of horseman her fiancé was and whether they could see the ring (you could spot it from the spires).

Finally, Woodman appeared across the hill. The groom led him gingerly, on a long lead shank, and as he turned into the stable and walked toward the show ring where we waited, Cross warned us about reaching out to touch. It seems he had bitten off the thumb of a stallion handler recently. Luckily, they found the thumb, and a French doctor who'd performed a hand transplant happened to be in town looking at horses, and he managed to reattach it.

When Woodman arrived before us, he stood as peacefully as any other stud. But his lips were covered with an unsightly green froth that made him look louche beyond redemption, like a sort of pasture-grazing Henry VIII. (During the spring, it's not unusual to see horses frothing after binging on sweet red and white clover; but there's no clover in January, and so no excuse for Woodman's current savage state.) It's absurd, of course, to expect a stallion to trouble himself about the fine points of personal appearance, and normally a groom might take care of such minor grooming matters. But right now, the world's most active stud couldn't get a soul to come near him.

There's not much frothing at the mouth in the Claiborne breeding shed. Gus Koch, the farm manager, is an ex–Marine sergeant, who came back from a tour of duty in Vietnam in 1968 and then started a family that grew to ten children. He knows about discipline, which he and his stallion manager, Jim Zajic, dole out in parental mixtures of encouragement and tough love. This is what they sound like when they have trouble with a hesitant young stallion:

> Zajic: Let's go. Get up.
> SMACK – an open-palm slap on the stallion's hind end.
> Zajic: Last three days he's been psycho. It's like he's forgot what he's doing.
> Koch (to the mare): Hold on, sister.
> Zajic: Get up, son.

In the middle of all the rearing and bellowing and heaving of loins, there's one quality that's easy to miss when you visit a breeding shed: how normal it all is to the people who work there. I finally pick up on this at Claiborne, just as they come to the end of the morning's work. Preach and Arch, Pulpit and Tough Broad have all come and gone, and the half-blind Danzig is eyeing his early appointment, Hidden Reserve, a stakes-winning Phipps mare who boards at the farm. There's nothing unusual about the way his interest quickly leads to action, and the old stallion has no trouble getting himself up on her back. While he's busy, Zajic, who holds Danzig's lead shank with one hand and the base of the stallion's penis with the other, stands almost shoulder to shoulder with Gus Koch, who waits by the mare's shoulder, firmly holding the leather strap that keeps her left foreleg in the air.

'The high-school superintendent is very pro-education,' Koch says.

'Oh, yeah?' Zajic says.

'See, because of the Kentucky education reform bill, every school's got a site-based council that makes the decisions now. But the problem is the school board still thinks they run the place.'

After the last mating – Horse Chestnut and Meadow Mist – Koch ducks into the lab to make a quick call home. He sat on the site-based council until recently and he still finds himself in the middle of its every crisis, including the latest, involving a feud between a powerful football coach and the high-school principal.

When you live on a farm, as Koch and his family do, it's hard to pinpoint where work ends and home life begins. Sometimes the overlap is comical. At the end of the day's breeding Koch shows me a 'dismount' in the microscope. A dismount is the last few drops of semen, which he catches in a plastic cup as the stallion backs off the mare. 'That's a pretty little sample, it don't really get any better than that,' he says. Koch started out on a Standardbred farm, so he's accustomed to handling samples. 'Used to take this stuff home with me. Shocked my mother-in-law once. I had this little sample sitting on the counter because I check for longevity. See how long it would live, you know. She didn't know what it was and made the mistake of asking.'

More often, running the farm and raising ten children fit neatly together, and as I follow Koch through his chores, he seems to consult not just with every barn on the three-thousand-acre farm but also with every civic governing body in a forty-mile radius. He's on the board of the Bourbon County hospital, he chairs the parish council, he directs the Farm Bureau and the Future Farmers of America, and so on. Koch speaks with the clipped phrasing of the man in charge and he has the honest man's habit of fixing you in the eye as he asks time-saving direct questions. He favors a no-muss, no-fuss haircut that's hard to catalogue but suits him perfectly: short, with a yesteryearly fringe of bowl-cut bangs across the forehead. The Caesar!

But as he gets away from the office and out into the fields, his conversation keeps turning back to his family. He tells me how easy it is to drop by the house and pick up a son to open the gates for him as he drives from pasture to pasture checking on the new foals. His second son, Steve, confirms this idyllic view of growing up on the Claiborne grounds. 'It's great for a boy to have a three-thousand-acre front yard. I don't think there's one stone on that farm that me and my brothers left unturned.'

It's not surprising to find out that all of the boys have taken an interest in horses. Charles, the oldest, works as a broodmare foreman on the farm. Matthew, who's now in the Marines, put himself through college as a blacksmith. Steve works as an associate director of sales at Keeneland. Anthony studies agricultural economics at the University of Kentucky. And everybody says Gus, the youngest, may be the best horseman of them all.

Out on the edge of Bourbon County, the Kochs have a seventy-acre place they call Mount Carmel. They keep some nurse mares and Percherons there, a few Thoroughbreds. 'In fact, we've got an Arch yearling that the boys and I are trying to raise,' Koch says, in the sort of dreamy tones that people use to talk about their vacation in Tuscany. 'I don't play golf. I love to farm. That's where I can get away and do something I enjoy.'

THIRTEEN

California Stud

C ᴇᴇ's Tɪᴢᴢʏ, ᴛʜᴇ sɪʀᴇ of Tiznow, the 2000 Horse of the Year and the only two-time winner of the Breeders' Cup classic, doesn't live in Kentucky. He plies his trade far from the bluegrass, at Harris Farms Horse Division, which is part of Harris Ranch, Inn and Restaurant, a fifteen-thousand-acre agricultural complex cum resort and steakhouse in Coalinga, California, in the San Joaquin Valley. 'Coalinga' sounds as if it could be a Native American word or a form of sexual acrobatics, but it is, in fact, a contraction of 'Coaling Station Λ', the name the place was given in 1891 by engineers of the Southern Pacific Railroad.

When Coalinga was incorporated, it was an oil boom town, with gambling-hall saloons, a famous madam, a Whiskey Row that served liquor all through Prohibition, and a gusher so big that, one Friday afternoon in November 1909, they closed down the LA Stock Exchange so that members could trot up to see it. Out on the oil leases, men had job titles like 'roughneck' and 'roustabout', and if they drilled for oil and got sulfur, they just set up a sulfur bath and charged admission. Two boom-town expatriates have gone on to fame outside Coalinga: the singer Jo Stafford, born in 1917 on Lease 35, who sang with Frank Sinatra and Tommy Dorsey; and Stanley (Frenchy) Bordagaray, who played for six Major League baseball teams in the thirties and forties, and once complained that the $500 fine he received for spitting on an umpire 'was a little more than I expectorated'.

Coalinga is a quiet town now, with a population of seven thousand or fifteen thousand, depending on whether you include the inmates at the Pleasant Valley State Prison and the Claremont Facility. It has one museum, the R. C. Baker Museum, where I learned all this local history from the curator, Helen Cowan, a contemporary of Jo Stafford's, who showed me the museum's display of a hundred and eighty varieties of barbed wire (to keep in cattle, not prisoners) and paused at a photo of Bordagaray's Whiskey Row saloon to say, 'I wish I had every dollar back that my dad spent there.'

Harris Farms is the biggest private employer in town. It's a huge place right off I-5, with a marquee you can see from about forty miles away. I have heard its location described variously as 'halfway between LA and San Francisco', 'halfway between the borders of Mexico and Oregon', and 'you can't miss it'. The seventy-foot-tall marquee looms over the interstate with a blinding taillight-red logo that seems to say, 'Congratulations, you've reached the middle of nowhere. Have a steak.'

For the inn and the restaurant, at least, the nearest competition is so far away that it isn't competition. The inn is an improbable oasis, a rambling pink hacienda arranged around the sort of Art Deco pool where Bogart would find the blonde after a long drive. There are palm trees and Jacuzzis, topiary in the shape of a teddy bear leading a horse, and barbed-wire swizzle sticks with the complimentary morning coffee. The restaurant across the parking lot is actually a mini-civilization made up of a bar, a gift shop, and three restaurants. The décor is equal parts racetrack photos and branding irons, lit by sprawling wrought-iron ranchero chandeliers.

John Harris, the owner and son of the founding rancher, Jack, is fifty-eight, with side-parted salt-and-pepper hair. He looks like a hawk, if hawks wore glasses and windbreakers and let themselves get a touch out of shape when things got busy. He walks with a waddle, like a man standing up after a long meal. He lives on the other side of the valley, near Sanger, and he flies himself to work, often switching the controls on his Cessna 210 to autopilot so he can read the papers. From the air, he can peek down at the valley's harlequin patchwork of crops and tell you which is romaine or almonds or garlic or red-leaf lettuce, or any of the other thirty-three things he grows. He keeps a hundred thousand head of cattle fattening on a feedlot. He calls himself 'kind of a micromanager', which in his case means that he eats meat at virtually every meal.

After we meet for breakfast (roast sliced tri-tip) at the Ranch Kitchen, Harris drives me over to the Horse Division. He takes I-5 and as he comes over a hill, all at once I see his hundred thousand cattle: it's like happening upon the March on Washington if everyone there weighed between seven hundred and a thousand pounds and slept in the mud. It also explains the scent I first picked up around the Olympic-sized pool, a scent I do not associate with either Bogart or blondes.

The Harris Farm setup differs from the standard one in Kentucky. Instead of wood fences, the paddocks are surrounded by oil-field pipes painted white. There's no fancy loading dock around the stallion station, because it just isn't practical to van into Coalinga for the day: mares going to a Harris stallion generally stay for the season. The farm sits on the alluvial soil of the San Joaquin floodplain, so the pasture is flat and the sense of distance is Western: you're surrounded by miles of valley and faraway mountains moving their shadows around all day. From his paddock, Cee's Tizzy, a gray horse, can look across the field-pipe fences to the mares with their new foals running lightly beside them. Most of the gray foals are his.

Harris Farm has its own track, where they train their own two-year-olds, who go out in sets of two or four or six with their exercise jockeys – a delightfully mismatched group consisting of a former real-estate saleswoman, a college student, an aspiring jockey, a racetrack veteran working his way back from drug suspension, and a former sitcom actor who never outgrew his child-star height. Everybody speaks English and Spanish in equal doses, even the Danish trainer, Per Antonsen, who sits on an exercise pony, watching the horses. The field beside the track is planted with acres and acres of garlic, so the horses race around the oval in a breeze rich with the smell of garlic greens.

The stallion paddocks are planted with fruitless mulberries that cover the place in cool shade. It's spring – a brief period after the winter fog and before the hills turn brown – so everything is green for a minute. Still there's lots of dirt, too. The horses like to roll in it, and when they stand up again, the dust rises off them in clouds, like steam.

It's not just the landscape that lets you know you're not in Kentucky: the mood on the California farm is different. Mexican workers do not act as if they're out of place. They sing *corridas* as they cut the lawn. Raul Rosas, who comes from Michoacán, started cutting lawns here sixteen years ago, and he runs the operation in the stallion barn now. And as the farm vet, Jeanne Bowers, palpates the mares, a guy in sunglasses, worn jeans, and cowboy boots with spurs comes jangling by. I ask the farm manager, Dave McGlothlin, what a cowboy's doing on a Thoroughbred farm. McGlothlin says the man's here to check on a sick mare, one of about a hundred saddle horses they use on the feedlot. He watches the cowboy go and offers his curt admiration: 'He's the real deal. He can ride and rope.'

John Harris's father, Jack, founded Harris Ranch in 1937; for the next few decades, he concentrated on growing cotton and grain. He didn't start messing with horses until the late fifties, and he didn't get serious about them until 1966, when, at his son's urging, the Harrises started keeping Thoroughbreds. John Harris got the bug when he took a summer job at AkSarBen Racetrack, in Omaha, Nebraska, in 1963. He fell in love with the whole backside atmosphere with its romantic cross section of Damon Runyon types, cowboys, trainers, tipsters, scam artists, silk suiters. 'Racing really gets in your blood,' he says. 'You get a passion for it.'

But Harris has to be a romantic in his spare time. For most of the day he's a twenty-first-century farmer. He drives past his broccoli and parsley and almonds, with one hand constantly punching numbers into his cell phone: to the office, to suppliers, to neighboring farms. He uses the word 'deal' a lot: 'Those are neat deals,' or 'It's a touchy little deal,' or 'We lost money on this organic deal'. It's a conversational tic, but it's also a way of life. Large-scale farming requires the brokering skills of a Beltway insider at budget time. When you're driving through the fifteen thousand acres with Harris, vegetables start to seem very dynamic.

At the end of the day, when he gets into his Cessna and flies back to River Ranch, his hundred-and-fifty-acre place on the eastern side of the valley, Harris can finally get romantic again. River Ranch is another world, lush and wild, with ancient sycamores and river oaks bending by an honest-to-God rushing river (the real gold in California). Other than the yearlings who are sent here for the rich pasture and the soft footing of the sandy soil, his nearest neighbors are bobcats, coyotes, and mountain lions – a combination that tends to legitimize the presence of the sighted rifle in the gun rack of the pickup driven by the River Ranch manager, Eric Smith. 'I work with horses because I don't do well with people,' the burly Smith says through his *Easy Rider* Fu Manchu mustache.

Harris's home is palatial, in the sense that it's a lot like a palace: marble floors with zebra skins, gold chinoiserie mirrors, blackamoor caryatids made of ebony, thematic murals painted on the walls and ceilings, an excitable rottweiler who responds to invisible commands. When Harris gets in, he pets the dog, kisses his wife, Carole, hello, drops off some paperwork, and goes out to look at the yearlings.

The Harris Farm yearlings live pretty much right outside the front door, and they're as beautiful as anything on the grounds. For horse lovers, yearlings are pretty irresistible. The colts are still coltish and the fillies are, too. They're playful, powerful, balanced, beautiful to look at; they're like da Vinci sculptures with the personalities of second graders. There are cynics who say that every horse is always for sale, but yearlings are horses at their most salable: they're young and unraced but old enough to hint at their true athletic potential. They're optimism on four legs.

They're also unnamed, which somehow adds to their allure. Buyers like to name their horses – the name is one of the few things about a horse that you can actually control. They name horses after girlfriends, hometowns, in-jokes, business deals. After the 2000 election, the Jockey Club, which must approve the name of every Thoroughbred, registered at least seven horses whose names contained the word 'chad'. Many names seem to be the result of a drunken impulse, and they stick around for a lifetime like a shore-leave tattoo. Names like Root Canal, Amputate, Bedpan, and Judge Smells set the gold standard in this category.

Farms with a lot of horses to christen try to come up with a system. Overbrook keeps a notebook around so folks can jot down a good one when the inspiration strikes, but if that fails they turn to the atlas for names like Flanders, Grand Canyon, Carson City, Idaho Falls. Claiborne prefers one-word, even one-syllable names, like Arch, Swale, Lure, Trip, Pulpit, Preach.

There are some basic rules that make the process a little like haiku. The names can be no more than eighteen characters long, including spaces and punctuation. Some owners try to sneak around this requirement, producing clumsy hustled-up names like Hoovergetthekeys or Shezafrequentflyer, which already sound like they're a few steps behind. Other names seem to laugh at the rule: Goooooooooooooooal. You can't use trademarks, and to name your horse after a living person you need permission. (One owner got approval to name his No Nukes colt Gorbachev by sending the United States Trotting Association, which follows the same rules as the Jockey Club, a note signed by an Officer Gorbachev who worked for a police force in Texas.)

There are no-brainer alternatives for the poetically challenged. People with a Storm Cat colt or filly try to throw either Cat or Storm into the name (Sharp Cat, Cyber Cat, Adcat; China Storm, Storm Broker). Whether they're being clever (Catillac), dull (Desert Stormer), or weird (Katz Me If You Can) is beside the point: the copycat name serves the same purpose as Louis Vuitton luggage, alerting the world that this cat has class.

The best names combine qualities of the sire and dam in a way that honors them – and if possible improves on the originals. When Judge Smells went to stud, a mare named Toronto Tea was bred to him: the resulting foal, Aromatic, recalls both the sire's ordure and the dam's bouquet. Certain studs are blessed with inspiring names. Poker was one: he sired Deal out of Joiner, Poking out of Merrymaking, Poke Salad out of Tom Sal, Hole Card out of Back Pocket, and Mist a Straight out of Foggy Crossing.

Certain owners and breeders, like Alfred Gwynne Vanderbilt and Seth Hancock's sister, Dell, are famous for the names they come up with, and John Harris would chuckle at the idea that he belongs in their company. He's a preoccupied and unpretentious man, comfortable with the corporate and the nondescript, a sort of Wallace Stevens of the Jockey Club Registry. He comes up with noble names (Blazing Skies), simple names (Flying), and great farm-bred names (Early Tomatoes). He got a lot of good names from the Harris Farm stallion Political Ambition: Soft Money, Early and Often, Work the Crowd. He's adept at playful references to the sire and dam. When he bred Nopro Blama to his stallion Moscow Ballet (son of Nijinsky, who was a son of Northern Dancer), he named the foal, born during the collapse of the USSR, Soviet Problem. When he bred his mare Talk Faster (out of Walk Faster) to Moscow Ballet, he named the 1997 filly Vodka Talking.

Giving names to the animals is good pastime for a man who lives in Eden, but apparently it's not one you can rush. Almost every day, Harris visits his yearlings when he comes home from work. Eric Smith often goes along with him. Harris checks out a few that look good enough to sell in the Del Mar Yearling Sale. Smith points out a suspicious hock or a turned-out knee and reports on eating habits. The conversation of the two men is businesslike but not urgent. They sound like a couple of concerned teachers trading stories in the teachers' lounge. Behind them, a pair of yearling colts bodyslam each other with NFL intensity, and the two men barely give it a glance.

It's not easy to be a stud outside Kentucky. Good homegrown mares usually gallop off to some famous Kentucky stallion, and the ones that do stick around for local service generally expect to get it cheap. This is true in forty-nine states – outside of the bluegrass there are no six-figure stud fees. Even though Cee's Tizzy's son (Tiznow) beat Storm Cat's son (Giant's Causeway) in the most important race of the year (the Breeders' Cup Classic) in 2000 (then became the only back-to-back Classic winner in 2001), Cee's Tizzy will not get a tenth of what Storm Cat does. He won't get a twentieth. Cee's Tizzy is lucky to get $15,000 a pop. Breeders will tell you that this is because Cee's Tizzy comes from a less than commercial family, and that Tiznow was something of a fluke. Other breeders will tell you he's just not fashionable. Who knows? Life is unfair, even for studs.

But there are ways of fighting back, however small and ineffectual. California has installed a sort of incentive program to encourage local breeding and to ensure that good mares keep bringing their business to California studs. It works like this: California racetracks run a slate of lucrative races restricted to native California horses, or 'Cal-breds'. Also, in certain races open to all comers, the state breeders' and owners' association add money to the purse if the winner is a Cal-bred. There are enough of these races to give owners an incentive to stock their stables with Cal-bred horses. In addition to these bonuses at the track, there are cash awards for the California stallions with the winningest group of offspring. For example, Cee's Tizzy, whose progeny earned $1,901,732 in qualifying races in 2000 (and earned $5,597,979 overall), got a $230,000 stallion award – a sizable dividend, more than fifteen times his stud fee. In theory, this encourages owners to stand their racehorses in California.

The sticking point in this program is how you define 'California bred', If you're too loose about it, and you say that a Cal-bred is any horse that happens to draw its first breath in California, then all the mares would ship out to Kentucky, breed to their studs, and return home only to drop their foals. This definition would in effect reduce the state's entire breeding population to a small group of females available only to out-of-state studs, a sort of Smith College effect. If, on the other hand, you're too strict about it, and you insist that the only horses that qualify as true Cal-breds are those born in California by a California stallion out of a California mare, then you impoverish your breeding stock, reducing your foal crop to inferior specimens bred by rejected stallions (since most states stock their stallion barns with studs that couldn't cut it in Kentucky) out of mares who aren't worth boarding in Kentucky.

This is how California solves the problem. A horse is considered Cal-bred if it is born in-state, by a California sire and dam, of course. But a foal may be also be called Cal-bred, even if its sire stands in another state, *if the dam is bred back to a California sire*. So, a son of

Storm Cat born in California won't be eligible for Cal-bred races unless his dam is bred back to, say, Cee's Tizzy. This fifty-fifty rule helps support the local breeding program two ways: it allows for local mare owners to improve their stock with occasional infusions from the world-class bloodlines stockpiled in Kentucky, and it helps support the stay-at-home studs and the breeders like Harris who manage them.

Cee's Tizzy has done well in the breeding shed, in spite of the sort of handicaps that overwhelm most mid-level, non-Kentucky stallions. He had the stud's typically equivocal race career: promising and short-lived. He ran well, winning half his starts, but he was big and prone to injury and he only raced six times. He sustained a slab fracture in his first Grade I, the Louisiana Super Derby, and retired to stud for the 1991 breeding season. During his first few years on the market, mare owners looked at his so-so race record and his pedigree (out of Chile on his dam's side and out-of-date on his sire's, where the highlight is his great-great-great-great-great-grandsire, Man O' War), and they took their business elsewhere. Cee's Tizzy ended up with a light workload of mostly downmarket mares – with the occasional good one sent over by his owner, Cecilia (Cee) Straub-Rubens, who didn't have to pay for the privilege.

In 1992, Cee bred Cee's Tizzy to Cee's Song, and got a big strong foal that she didn't like enough to keep: in his first start, she entered the horse, Budroyale, in a claiming race (in England, claiming races have a more straightforward name: 'selling races'), and somebody snatched him up. Budroyale went on to place second in the 1999 Breeders' Cup Classic, behind Cat Thief. But Straub-Rubens, who'd learned by then to like the mating, kept sending Cee's Song to Cee's Tizzy, and in 1997, she got the foal she was looking for, Tiznow, a surviving twin. (The vet who performed the selective abortion says, 'Looking back, I guess that I pinched the right one.')

On the farm, Tiznow was a big rough colt who beat up on his playmates. On the track, he bullied the best horses in the world.

Tiznow's race career proves that there can be unexpected advantages when a horse is bred by an unpopular sire and out of an unfashionable family. His owners, Straub-Rubens and Michael Cooper, turned down an offer of $5 million to retire him in 2000 – a lowball figure for a Horse of the Year, $55 million less than the final offer for Fusaichi Pegasus, who placed sixth, eight lengths behind him, in the Breeders' Cup. Cooper, who's a financial adviser, turned up his nose at the money and sent Tiznow back to the glory of the track. 'If you want to make money, you invest in stock or real estate,' he said. 'The sport needs more stars, not more stallions.' He repeated the verdict the day after Tiznow won in 2001, saying 'Is there a rule against three? If Tiznow is sound we want to go for another year. He's a racehorse.' A few days later, though, he came to his financial senses, retiring Tiznow to WinStar Farm in Versailles, Kentucky. WinStar set his stud fee at $30,000, a recession-era figure low enough to attract mares of quality

After Tiznow's first victory, Cee's Tizzy's stud fee rose from $7,500 to $15,000, and his mares improved in quality and quantity, a change that has had little effect on his standard of living. Most of the time, Cee's Tizzy hangs out, as he has for the past ten years, on the mountain side of the stallion barn, the first paddock on his right after he leaves his stall. According to his trainer, John Russell, he was rambunctious at the track, the sort of high-energy horse who liked to run so much and so hard that he practically trained himself. He's mellowed with retirement.

At just fourteen, Cee's Tizzy is a gray horse gone white with age. Around the farm, they call him the Gray Horse and sometimes the Big Horse, because, while Cee's Tizzy may be a suitable name for a plaything, it's rather undignified for a leading sire. His color is officially gray. But the official colors for the registry gray, bay, black, chestnut – are like racial categories on the census: they don't begin to describe the complex shades of real individuals. From a distance and out in the open, the Gray Horse is bright white, like oil paint fresh from the tube, but up close, he's covered with tiny black freckles. His eyes and lips are coal black, as if his inner nature were contrary to what you see, and as he walks under the mulberries, the shade of the leaves blends in with the shadows of his muscles and the bright white of his coat flashing in the sun, and, amazing as it sounds, he can be hard to spot, like a ghost in broad daylight.

Seeing him in the breeding shed strips away some of the mystery. The Harris Farm shed is huge, square, with a high steel roof that keeps the place cool. Because the walls are unpadded, mare and stallion mate in the middle of the floor, doors wide open, instead of pressed against the wall the way they do in Kentucky, so the mare can't run. Dave McGlothlin preps the mare, doubling her tail inside a see-through plastic glove and taping the glove down so it doesn't fall off, a precaution that prevents a long, sharp, stray hair from working its way into the act, getting stuck and causing lacerations. Imagine getting a twenty-two-inch paper cut when you least expect it.

McGlothlin waits beside the mare, Elegant Beauty, and Rosas brings in the Gray Horse, who seems eager, even anxious, as if he's known a few who got this far and then just up and left. He's not pawing at the ground in barely contained violence, the way Dynaformer and Storm Boot do; he's taking tiny steps and staying in one place, as if he has to pee. For all his pacing, he's not ready yet, and Rosas snaps his lead shank, which seems to work. The Big Gray stops jittering around and stands quietly for a moment, like a diver on the high dive.

Once he's ready, he rises up, prancing forward to tuck himself in, and he lets out a giggle. I'm not making this up – it's a giggle, three or four counts, high-pitched, nervous, leaving an impression of antic and inappropriate glee. I have come to expect big rebel yells at the moment of impact, vicious and terrifying, leaving an impression of what you might politely call 'macho bullshit', so this giggle is about as surprising as anything I've witnessed in the breeding shed. But why shouldn't he giggle? All of a sudden, he's one of the busiest stallions in California. He's the first one who sounds like he recognizes the goofy good luck of it all: he's Hef, only young and without the editorial responsibilities.

'He's normally a quicker worker than that,' McGlothlin says when the Gray Horse comes back to earth. I ask about the giggle, and they all seem to think it's normal.

FOURTEEN

The Eloquent Stud

THERE'S NOTHING LIKE gossiping about sirelines with an experienced breeder. On a slow hot Saturday in the northern California delta region south of Stockton, Duane Griffith, the farm manager of Applebite Farms, leans against the hood of the farm's pickup truck. 'The Seattle Slews are known to be cryptorchids,' he says, raising an eyebrow to see if I'm familiar with the technical term for horses with an undescended testicle. He offers a couple examples: A. P. Indy, Slew O'Gold. And the knock on the Northern Dancer line, he tells me, is that the stallions aren't fertile. 'Cigar, see, he's got the Northern Dancer line.' We remember some others who shot mostly blanks: Storm Bird; El Gran Señor; the totally sterile $10.2-million yearling, Snaafi Dancer.

'On the other hand, the Raise a Native-line stallions are really prolific, semen-wise,' Griffith says. We talk in the shade a while about such matters.

Outside Kentucky, breeders rarely get their hands on the latest multiple stakes winner, the headline grabber hot off the track. Instead, they tend to land horses a generation removed from the spotlight: the top stallions at Applebite Farm are Distinctive Cat, an unraced son of Storm Cat; and Western Fame, a son of Gone West who won a few times, but apparently not enough to attract a Kentucky clientele. With such good-looking ne'er-do-wells in the stallion barn, Applebite has to use a different marketing strategy.

While Coolmore, with a roster stocked with Kentucky Derby winners, can sell mare owners on a stallion's track record, Applebite is more likely to talk about the traits of a stud's illustrious family.

'I haven't seen any other Storm Cats but I guarantee you he's probably the best-looking Storm Cat in California,' Griffith says, as we watch Distinctive Cat proudly patrolling the fenceline in his half-acre paddock. 'Yeah, I'll put him up against any of them, you know, as far as looks are concerned. And his babies are extremely good-looking, too.' In fact, the Cat, as he's known on the farm, is handsome to the point of prettiness: a brilliantined black horse with four white stockings, a big sidewinding blaze, and the sort of sculpted physique that you normally associate with guys who train in front of mirrors. 'Even a veteran horseman looks at him and thinks, *Brick shithouse*,' Griffith says.

The Cat keeps himself busy. He seems to run both for the sound of it – the pleasing echo of his own hoofbeats on the loamy delta soil – and the look of it, as when he cuts suddenly, whipping his head around and tossing his mane. But in the middle of his show paces, he stops and ambles mildly over to the fence. He comes right up, sticks his head over the railing, and begins nudging me until I pet his nose – surprisingly mild-mannered and unsuspicious behavior for a stallion.

'He's a friendly spirit,' Griffith says. 'He's very easy to get along with. Wish they were all as easy as him.'

Griffith is pretty friendly himself. He talks with a Texas drawl and doesn't hurry through a conversation, and while he's waiting for the next thing to say, he seems to do a lot of noticing. I'm not surprised when he mentions hunting back in Texas; he has the steady blue eyes and wary contentment of the retired gunslinger. He started working in California just before breeding season, and in the entire three months since, he has left Applebite's hundred acres just once, for a day trip to the foothills sixty miles away. 'You're kind of in your own world here,' he says. 'What it does, it makes you not want to leave.'

Applebite sits at the corner of French Camp Road and Airport Way, two busy streets in a way station of a town fifteen miles from south Stockton. Even city boosters would call south Stockton the bad end of town, with its depopulated expanses of power plants, warehouses, light industry, and truck lots. The standard metropolitan sprawl is creeping into French Camp, too, and threatening the local agriculture: UPS built a sorting center just down the road, the mayor of Stockton wants to expand the airport just five miles from Applebite, and long-range commuters from Oakland and San Francisco are starting to eye the local housing.

But once you're on Applebite Farms, you'd barely suspect any of that. True, twenty minutes into my first tour, I hear the screech and crash of a semi and an SUV on the corner of French Camp and Airport Way, followed by the sound of sirens. But that's what it takes – a teenager sideswiping a tractor trailer and rolling his parents' car – to make you think of the world beyond the pampas grass, the thick blackberry bushes and poplar trees, the converted prewar dairy barns, the wisteria growing on the gazebo, the old red Chevy flatbed truck with the big fifties fenders piled high with straw.

The small farm runs efficiently, and the mares in heat line up for palpations as they do on every breeding farm. But there's a fairytale quality at Applebite that you don't find on bigger places. For instance, over the palpation chute, I spot a dreamcatcher, one of those supposedly Native American contraptions of sticks and strings and feathers that you can buy at crafts fairs and bookstores that specialize in meditation paraphernalia. I ask Griffith, who's got a plastic glove on to help with palapations, if he hung it there.

'No, I did not,' he says emphatically, then softens his answer a bit: 'I guess it's kind of appropriate, though. Where dreams are made.'

The next day, Joan Rogers, a probate and estate-planning lawyer in Santa Clara and the owner of Applebite Farms, comes to visit the new foals and yearlings. I had 'met' Rogers months before, when she e-mailed a detailed and scholarly answer to a bloodline question I'd sent to an online forum, and we later had a deeply academic battle over my use of the word 'stud' (among other things, I'd asked whether anyone knew where Lexington, the famous nineteenth-century 'blind stud', had gone during the Civil War; she chided me for using 'stud' as a synonym for 'Thoroughbred stallion', since the word properly describes only the establishment where Thorough-breds breed). Apart from her presence on the Thoroughbred Heritage site, Rogers participates in a very active equine-science discussion group – the trainers and vets discuss alternative treatments that might be dismissed in other parts of the country, like whether horses, who don't really exercise that much, should be trained harder, using some of the scientific methods and cross-training techniques applied to Olympic athletes. In the hidebound, tradi-tional world of Thoroughbred racing, you don't have to go too far to be considered pretty out there.

Rogers's father, a dentist and frustrated dairyman, bought the place in 1939; it was a dairy farm then. Her mother, who'd gone along with the purchase, paid off the mortgage while he was off fighting the war; they divorced when he returned, and she got the farm in the settlement. But she wasn't a frustrated dairyman, so she rented it, and for the next fifty years not a lot changed at Applebite, except that the pastures got overgrazed, the tenants started taking wood from the roof of the long barn to fix things elsewhere, the well stopped working, and the wiring went.

When her mother died, in 1994, Rogers decided to turn Applebite into a Thoroughbred breeding farm. She had it painted and rewired; she bought an aerator; she found a used manure spreader up in a farm in Saskatchewan to fix the soil. She put in the gazebo and wisteria. She planted two hundred trees every year.

Rogers has always ridden, and she seems to have read every book about horses, from the *Black Stallion* books of her girlhood to the rare historical treatises she now hunts down through foreign booksellers and online auctions. So when she set about acquiring bloodstock for her farm, she already knew her way around. 'This is what we tried to do with Cat and with Western Fame,' she tells me. 'Buy horses that we thought had enough pedigree, and enough other good things that we could say about them, and present them with mares that would complement their good qualities – and to focus on a regional market. I mean, we know we're not going to go back and compete with Coolmore, we're just trying to bring good bloodlines cost-effectively to California breeders.'

On average, California horses run more over longer careers. This is mostly an unintentional virtue: since nobody's paying six-figure fees for the chance to send their mares to a Cal-bred stallion, good horses stay longer at the track. As a result, California is closer to the traditional economics of racing: horses are valuable here because thay make money racing, and stud fees tend to reflect the offsping's chances of winning a few times. Even though this is a sort of traditionalism by default, the greater emphasis on sport is real. California tends to breed with an eye on the racetrack, Kentucky with an eye on the sales.

As she visits the foals and yearlings, Rogers takes digital snapshots to post on the Applebite website and talks over sales prospects and breeding plans with Griffith. She wears running shoes and a pale blue linen painter's smock, and from time to time she does betray the enthusiasms of the Sunday watercolorist – avidness and susceptibility to inspiration – but the running shoes are not for show. She marches through the whole hundred acres, checking on every horse individually and greeting new foals with a little of their family history and a precise rundown of their conformational flaws. She's direct and affectionate with horses out of lifelong habit. She tells one mare, 'You have a lovely, rascally little daughter.' And to a Distinctive Cat foal who keeps nudging her shoulder and nipping needily at her, she says sharply, 'Artie, you're a pest, do you know that?'

Rogers points out a little whirlpool of a cowlick down the bridge of one foal's nose and cites a book about the interpretation of such markings, by Linda Tellington-Jones, a holistic trainer who pioneered the use of bodywork techniques on horses. 'The Japanese won't buy a horse if the cowlick is below the eye,' Rogers says. 'They think they're mean.' She points out another foal with big eyes. 'Great big eyes are supposedly representative of kindness, intelligence, generosity of spirit. Arabians have that. And the small eyes are known as pig eyes, which indicate stupidity, bad temper. Some mustangs have that.' She doesn't seem to be endorsing the ideas she brings up, as much as flipping through an index of approaches catalogued over a lifetime of study guided by the following principle: if it's about horses, I'll read it.

I ask her whether she's read Jane Smiley's *Horse Heaven* – she has – and whether she knows anyone like the psychic in the novel who could talk to horses and tell what they were thinking. She says she does, in fact, know the name of a telepathic animal communicator.

At about three o'clock, we head toward the breeding shed – there's one mare ready, scheduled for Western Fame – and Rogers mentions another theory she's unearthed. 'Supposedly, there's a pH change in the uterus after four in the afternoon that makes it more likely to have a filly. And last year our vet was overworked and we did breed a lot after four' – the vet couldn't get to the farm any earlier – 'and we did have a lot of fillies.'

But I didn't come to Northern California to see Western Fame, and I'm a little disappointed that there are no mares ready for the Cat. I have to console myself with watching the stallion groom, Dave King (if I forget his name, I can just look down at his giant

DAVE belt buckle), giving the Cat the deluxe trim for an afternoon photo shoot. He pulls out the Electro-Groom, with booster power – a sort of giant Dustbuster cum horse shaver – and starts hoovering his coat. King sympathizes with my bad luck, but, he tells me, the Cat has 'bred just about everything on the farm. First time he's had two days off in his life'. I sit on a hay bale as he finishes up with the mane, which he trims by taking a handful and yanking. 'You don't cut anything with scissors. It doesn't look natural.' Except for the yanking, King's hands move in the deft and gentle style of hair-dressers everywhere.

A few weeks after my visit, Rogers e-mails me the number of the telepathic animal communicator, Raphaela Pope. I'm still disap-pointed about missing Distinctive Cat in the breeding shed, but I realize that Pope can help me. If I can't see the Cat working in the shed, maybe I can ask him about it.

Pope is a former nurse – she logged more than twenty years in intensive-care and critical-care units – who's been a full-time telepath for the past six years. 'Nursing develops great compassion and empathy and allows you to project yourself into the *other's* situation,' she says. Apparently, one thing telepathy has over nursing is that you don't have to leave home to do it; Pope now does most of her projecting over the phone. It works like this: a pet owner, or what Pope refers to as the 'animal's person', calls her, usually in a panic because the animal is lost or sick, and Pope 'tunes in' to the animal, getting pictures that she translates into words. For instance, Rogers first called Pope when her dog, Helga, got a cut on the ear, requiring stitches. She wanted to know how Helga cut herself. According to her website, Pope tuned in and Helga 'showed me a picture of digging at the wooden fence surrounding her property. Several inches down Helga tried to get her face under the fence, only to run into an old rusty piece of barbed wire. A few days later Joan called to tell me that she had asked Helga to show her exactly where the wire was. Helga led her to the spot and Joan found the old rusty wire wrapped around the base of the fence!' Rogers was so wowed by the incident that she now calls Pope occasionally for help with her horses. ('It's hard to talk about things that are not provable scientifically,' Rogers said of her skeptical interest in Pope's communiqués. 'Whatever the reality, it gives me another avenue to think about.')

Despite logistical complications (I have to call Pope with questions, then Pope calls Rogers to tune in, then I call Pope back to get the answers), reaching Distinctive Cat proves a lot easier than dealing with most famous interview subjects, Michael Jordan, say, or Britney Spears. Although Pope ends up rewriting some of my questions, Distinctive Cat seems unaware of this, and he answers with the freshness and lack of suspicion typical of those who have never been interviewed.

> Interviewer: Are you conscious of being a special or privileged horse?
>
> The Cat: Of course.
>
> (Pope interrupts her telepathy here to laugh like crazy at his answer.)
>
> Distinctive Cat: Of course. Yes, I do understand that. I have always been in a special position – but not all the horses here have been. I came in sort of expecting to go to the track. [Distinctive Cat had the offset knees typical of the sons of Storm Cat, but because of a complication in the orthopedic procedure designed to correct it, he never got to run.] I did expect to go to the track, and I wanted to. But it's not so bad the way it's worked out.

In my original questions, I wanted to know whether Distinctive Cat knew about Storm Cat, whether he was aware of his relationship to the leading sire, but Pope says that when she asked, he got confused and said, '*I'm* the Cat.' She didn't take it any further.

Interviewer: What do you think of your life as a stallion at Applebite?

The Cat: It's very pleasant here. I'm very well treated. It's a very good life. There are some restrictions, of course.

Interviewer: Oh? Tell me about that. What are the restrictions?

The Cat: This is not some wild-range situation where I have my own herd, and we, the horses, kind of manage everything. No, you have to cooperate with the humans. There are artificial aspects of it, but on the whole it's fine.

At this point in the interview, Pope and Rogers chatted and decided to add a more general question, to give Distinctive Cat an opportunity to say something personal about his life – a word or two from the horse's mouth.

The Cat: Well, Thoroughbred horses have been bred for centuries to run. It's what we love to do. But it's only part of a horse's life. There are many other pleasures.

Interviewer: And what are those pleasures?

The Cat: Well, rolling in the dirt, for example. And cats, for example.

According to Rogers, whom Pope quotes at this point, Distinctive Cat does, in fact, love watching the barn cats who roam in and around his stall. But she suddenly ends the audio transmission and instead begins describing the 'picture' that Cat 'gave her'. Pope tells me that he showed her his groom – the reader should picture a skinny guy with a big DAVE belt buckle who plays a lot of classic rock on the barn radio – taking him out of his stall, while the Cat himself dances along at the end of his lead line, going out, presumably, to be admired and petted by those who stop by. Pope ends the interview with the Cat's final words, his take on the simple pleasures of being a stud. 'You know,' he says through his interpreter. 'Just dancing along and being petted. I like it all.'

FIFTEEN

New Mexico Stud

'FOR THIRTY-TWO YEARS, I've worked with inferior horses,' Loren Bolinger, the owner of Running Horse Farm, says. 'When a customer drives up with a van, I know it's an inferior horse.' Bolinger, who, with his wife, Nancy, and one farmhand, does all the work on his twenty-five-acre stud farm in Albuquerque, on the banks of the Rio Grande, is a recreational grouser. In the two days I spend with him, he grouses about people, people from California, people from North Albuquerque, people from east of the Mississippi. He grouses about lowlife contractors; knucklehead employees and their tales of woe; the president, who reminds him of assholes he went to high school with; the county officials who want him to take his business indoors ('Some folks, for modesty reasons, have their eyes veiled from such carnal activities as stallions breeding mares'); the bureaucracy of the American Quarter Horse Association; the weak engines of late-model cars.

But just because he enjoys complaining doesn't mean he isn't right about his horses. Subfertile mares tend to migrate from good farms in Kentucky and California to regional markets. The culls who can't conceive with regularity wind up passing through a broodmare sale at Keeneland and shipping out to places like Running Horse Farm, where Bolinger has been scratching by on rejects since the early Nixon administration. 'We're having to deal with a lot of mares that would not pass scrutiny at better breeding farms,' Bolinger says. 'And I have to make my bones on those subfertile mares.'

It's not just the inferior mares he's mad about. 'They'll sell you a goddamn stud that isn't worth – ' By 'they', Bolinger means Kentucky horsemen. 'If he's not good enough to stand back there, then they figure that we'll take him. You know, if a stud is not good enough, he's not good enough to stand anywhere. But they'll sell us these horses that are unraced, unplaced, and ugly. Or have goofy bloodlines. Or they'll sell us a grass horse even though we're a dirt state. Or sell us a horse that has European stamina in a land where we have a lot of sprints.' Bolinger deals with the untrustworthiness of Kentucky horsemen the way most people deal with the weather: he complains, then does the best he can.

His good fortune in recent years is relative: Running Horse's big success, Devil Begone, carries the cheapest stud fee, $2,000, of any horse in this book – still enough to make him almost the most expensive stallion in New Mexico, just shy of Prospector Jones and Danzatore, who command $3,000 each, and Poles Apart, at $2,500. But Devil Begone's rise to such heady company has to be balanced against the calamitous end of Look See, Bolinger's best stallion in his thirty-two years of operation, and the only one near good enough to sell back up the ladder to Kentucky. That dream ended in catastrophe, at 4:45 AM, August 8, 1999, when, on a perfectly calm night, a tree toppled in Look See's paddock, crushing him instantly.

Bolinger, a counterculture curmudgeon who wears his gray ponytail tied back with a hair twistie and reminisces to the seventeen-year-old who delivers the hay about the Summer of Love ('before social diseases and all these bad drugs'), is the only Thoroughbred owner I've met to use the rhetoric of class warfare in a discussion of breeding. 'These boys come to Keeneland in their 747s that they leave idling at the Blue Grass Airport, and they buy their horses. And all us mortals try to assess what the hell the crazy prices really mean. You know, the rich, the truly rich, are above all economy. Even war doesn't affect them, if they're really rich. They're so wealthy that they are above all but the most extreme kind of thing that could happen in life.'

Bolinger and his horses are not. The farm's office and only residence (apart from a shed where the Mexican farmhand stays with his wife) is a double wide mobile home; the horses live under the open sky on dirt plots no bigger than a Levittown kitchen, an arrangement Bolinger calls 'the feedlot system'. The foaling barn was made in 1947 out of stacks of leftover ammo boxes ('25 round-shell high-explosive M54'). A rubber hose, of the sort you used to see in gas stations in the days before self-serve, stretches across the entrance to the farm; a bell dings when a car or horse van rolls over it. Bolinger says, 'We can't do what they do on a fancy Kentucky farm. The customers aren't going to pay for landscaping in their horse bills.'

Luckily, the landscaping is already there: the farm sits on the edge of the Rio Grande, on bosky bottomland between the Manzano and the Sandia Mountains to the east and the north and, sharply rising to the west, the start of mesa land. Craggy old cottonwoods, *los álamos*, tower over the foaling barn and beyond the muckpile on the part of the property where Bolinger keeps some horse vans, truck parts, and one of his collection of seventies-era Lincolns. The land by the river faces a wilderness preserve, and some nights when Bolinger comes out at three o'clock in the morning to irrigate his alfalfa field, he says there are so many damn animals running around that there ought to be a traffic light. The horses – five stallions, four yearlings, two two-year-olds, a pony horse, and twenty-two mares, many with a foal beside them – seem to fit in this landscape, like a remuda resting by the river in the middle of a cattle drive, huddled so close together that their snorts and blows and stirrings pass through the herd like a shudder through the body or wind over the tall grass.

The farm's name, Running Horse, is something of a misnomer, since even the biggest of the horse pens – Devil Begone's – doesn't have much more than two strides of running room. A more accurate name would be Bucking Horse Farm or Running Full Speed Into the Oil-Field Pipes Farm. Still, even in such cramped quarters, the Thoroughbreds manage to show off their athleticism. For instance, when Bolinger takes the teaser, Tilt the Odds, a well-bred regional stallion who's not pulling in the mares he used to, to check on each mare who still has to be bred, the 'open' ones who aren't in the mood right now practically pirouette in disgust, their hind legs whipping up just clear of the top pipe, or nicking it a little – on purpose? – so the iron fencing rings in warning and the whole movable setup of pens shakes. Tilt the Odds, who's used to these flamencolike displays of fury, just heads down the line.

'You use an older stallion like that for a teaser, it's almost like he's talking to you,' Bolinger says. On the other side of the pen, Nancy Bolinger holds a clipboard to keep track of who's in heat and who's not. As Tilt the Odds goes nose to nose nuzzling the eager mares, Nancy checks the other end for winking, which she calls beeping – the wink-wink rhythm and the mare's tendency to back up in the process reminds her of heavy-duty equipment going in reverse. Nancy is catlike: she has a wide catlike face and is given to mysterious catlike silences, even under direct questioning. In conversation, it's easy to get a sense of her sixties antiestablishment style. For instance, when I ask her if she's a New Mexico native, she waits awhile before saying, 'No, I'm straight.' Then she waits some more before telling me that she comes from 'western occupied New York' – the sort of answer I'd expect to get from Cinque of the Symbionese Liberation Army or from John Lennon on a press-shy day.

While this teasing is going on, another stallion, Highland Park, a recent transfer from Pine Brook Farm, in Warrenton, Virginia, seethes, racing back and forth in his pen and smashing into the fence. All this nuzzling and courtship right under his nose – the teaser is dallying with mares less than ten yards away – enrages him; he bellows like Brando in *Streetcar* and rams his chest into the welded iron again and again, a scene of frustration he has enacted so many times in his three months of residence that he's knocked the paint off the fence. But except to give him a wide berth as they walk by, Nancy, Loren, and Tilt the Odds barely notice the shenanigans. 'That teaser is getting him fit,' Bolinger says.

The daily flirtation tour with the teaser stallion cuts down on vet bills; most of the Bolingers' clients can't pay for the combination of palpation and ultrasound that's standard on the big Kentucky farms. He tells me that his low-tech method translates into a 40 per cent conception rate on the first cover (the standard in Kentucky is well over 60 per cent), but his stallions aren't too busy to fit in a follow-up session with their mares. Out here in New Mexico, the old-fashioned way works just fine.

As a result of the tour, the twelve-year-old mare Patty O'Furniture lands a date with Devil Begone. Whenever Bolinger talks about Devil, he drops his dark Old Testament tone and turns into a fan: 'That horse is a reincarnation of Alydar,' he says, comparing the stallion to his maternal grandfather, the Hall-of-Fame racehorse who accomplished something no other horse ever has: he finished a close second to the eventual Triple Crown winner Affirmed in all three races. (After the two horses retired to stud Alydar exacted his revenge: *he* turned into an expensive and prepotent sire, and Affirmed lagged far behind.) In case I find the comparison far fetched, Bolinger adds, 'Often you see inheritance zigzag through the pedigree.'

Bolinger is a fanatical student of pedigrees, and he takes every opportunity to expound on his theories. He leans on one of the four rusted Mark IVs in the part of his yard he's turned into a Lincoln sanctuary, and he says, 'Lord Derby represents the most elemental truth about breeding theory.' He pronounces the name 'Darby' in the proper English fashion. He prints out a few hundred pages of his writings on the subject, and we sit on his front steps while he explains his inscrutable pedigree diagrams. He has to be this fanatical. In a land of barren mares and hand-me-down stallions, hunting for a magic combination of hybrid bloodlines is how he gets an edge. He even sees his work in a philanthropic light. He talks about 'repairing the bloodlines' and 'returning the mare to elite productivity'. He can sound like a crackpot, but he still may be right. 'If hybrids bred true,' he says, 'only kings and queens would own horses.'

After a while, it becomes clear that his gruffness hides the sort of logic-resistant optimism that can weather heartbreaks — a valuable trait in a horseman. Clearly he's already transferred his affections from Look See to his new top stud. 'This horse has a spooky ability to correct conformational flaws,' he tells me, assuring me that Devil Begone can get good-looking babies out of crooked mares. If he's right, Devil could be mighty busy in these parts.

The Devil's downside, however, is that he's mean. He's a dark bay horse with an unbrushed coat and a mane that hangs down in long, wild clumps like dreadlocks because he's too mean to groom. 'That horse, when he's pissed off, his eyes burn like dark red coals, his ears disappear, and all's you can see are teeth and front feet,' Bolinger says. Stallions with a bad attitude often get sold down the river the way subfertile mares do, and places like Running Horse are left to oversee the mating of the mean with the hopeless. 'What I learned with this horse especially, but I know in all stallions,' he says, 'you establish a routine, and then you never, ever vary one bit. Now we always breed him exactly the way we done here. It doesn't look like much, but yet there's a pattern that he agrees with and he likes, and he and I have kind of mutually agreed that it's safe and we can deal with.'

Nancy leads Patty O'Furniture past the rest of the mares to Devil. She lets the two horses consort awhile over what Bolinger calls 'the Old English teasing wall', a few yards of weathered boards covering a corner of the fence. During this distraction, Bolinger respectfully enters Devil's paddock with a soft and raggedy cotton lead shank ('Don't be fighting me. Who brings you the mares, dude?') and when his stallion's excited enough he clips the shank to the halter and leads Devil out to the paltry shade of the cottonwood.

The farmhand tightens the twitch, and Nancy puts a reassuring hand on the bright white Patty O'Furniture, who favors the same Rasta style that Devil does but couples the look with a sweeter disposition. Patty's been through this procedure before – she's had a few good New Mexico runners, like Paddy O'Party and Fromout-ofheclouds – and she braces herself and waits. Bolinger and his wife both hold the leads loosely, even negligently: if either horse felt like making a run for it, here's the chance.

Running is not what they feel like doing. 'Now watch how he mounts this mare,' Bolinger says, a sexual safari guide dressed in dainty wrist-length latex gloves. 'He'll pick himself up' – Devil stands on his hind legs and rests his right foreleg on Patty's back with gentlemanly delicacy – 'and then he'll spread himself on the mare.' For one Mother-may-I moment, Devil lies on Patty O'Furniture's back, a startling gesture, but just the sort of tenderness you some-times run into in a mean stud that the rest of the world gave up on. After the permission he seems to be asking for is granted, he bites down on her neck and hangs on. When he's finished, he has a fuzzy white streak down his dark chest, little shedded clumps of her winter coat, and he goes back to his pen in peace with a long flossy strand of her mane stuck in his teeth.

SIXTEEN

Stud in the Wild:
The Harem Stallion

I T ' S R A I N I N G , T H E first hard rain of spring, and I'm standing in the middle of a herd of wild horses. Usually, this herd scatters over the countryside into five separate harems and a bachelor band, each with its own mood and rank in the hierarchy, but in the driving rain, they've come closer together, sixty-two horses – Shetland ponies, actually – setting aside their squabbling for a while to huddle near the top of a hill. They turn their butts to the driving rain, and as the wind shifts, the herd shifts with it, like a weathervane.

The herd lives about thirty miles west of Philadelphia, in Kennett Square, Pennsylvania, shuttling around from field to field at the New Bolton Center, a thousand-acre preserve and veterinary facility owned by the University of Pennsylvania. Despite the closeness of the research labs and large-animal hospital, the ponies live with almost no human intervention: they're never stabled, receive no food (except for small amounts in deep winter), and undergo virtually no medical treatment. They mate, give birth, struggle with each other, and die all on their own, under the open sky.

Still, they're used to having people around, mostly vet students and researchers from the Havemeyer Equine Behavior Lab, who come out to the fields to observe: to wander among them checking for new foals, charting copulatory frequency, monitoring power struggles, and puzzling over the habits of the harem stallions. As a rule, the healthy harem stallion is fertile and ready when called upon. Various stallions have been observed fulfilling harem duties two times in seven minutes; twenty-four times in a day; three times in an hour; and, on one occasion, with two mares three times each in a two-hour period. Even in slow times, they keep themselves busy with a form of inscrutable social commentary known as stud piles: prancing eagerly from one fecal pile to the next, they inspect fresh deposits and form their own response, sometimes alone, sometimes in lively one-on-one exchanges with rival stallions. Wherever you go, especially along fence lines, by gates, or in the middle of common paths, you step over the record of their debates.

Although I've called them wild horses, that's actually a misnomer. In fact they're semiferal ponies. To be picky about it (as breeders are), the wild horse became extinct sometime after 1969, when the last of the wild Przewalskis was spotted near a spring in Gum Tanga at the Mongolian edge of the Gobi desert. Today, all herds of 'wild' horses – the Camargue in the salt marshes of southern France, Kiger mustangs on Steens Mountain in Oregon, Exmoor ponies on the Cumbrian Fells in north England – descend from domestic horses gone feral, or, in the case of the Przewalskis, from a few surviving zoo animals who were reintroduced to the steppes west of Ulaan-baatar in 1991, and taught how to survive in the wild by Dutch preservationists.

The herd I'm standing in is classified as semiferal. Feral herds are supposedly untended and unconfined, with minimal contact with humans, while semiferal ones live in more closely managed pre-serves, like these fields in Kennett Square. All herds are maintained in some manner, either culled or augmented by the people who manage them, and these managers, usually from agencies like the

Bureau of Land Management or the Foundation for the Preservation and Protection of the Przewalski Horse, shape the migrations of the herds and determine their range.

The Kennett Square ponies spend much of the year by a slow-moving stream ringed with fields and woods, but from time to time they have to seek other pastures. Their spring camp is a twenty-five-acre field of tall, fresh grass by the New Bolton swine unit and dairy. Right now, the swine (part of an experiment in cloning hearts from fetal pigs, a first step in the effort to grow organs for transplant) are nowhere to be seen. There's a flock of lambs coming and going on the next hill over, and you can spot a cow or two lying down in the pasture beyond that, but otherwise the hills are deserted. It even takes a while to spot the herd, who've tucked themselves into the farthest corner of their current running grounds, by an old run-in shed on the crest of the hill.

This herd's been growing since 1994, when Sue McDonnell, the veterinary researcher who heads the Havemeyer Equine Behavior Lab, started acquiring Shetland ponies from local farms and auctions and turning them out to live year-round on their own. Since 1995, no new horses have come from outside. More than half the current herd was born in the wild – or the semiwild, or whatever you call the horses' self-governed life here in their own gated community.

I walk slowly through the herd, skirting the different groups with deference. They may be ponies, but even the smallest adult weighs well over four hundred pounds, and they're tough, part of a breed originally exported from the Shetland Islands, north of mainland Scotland and west of Norway, to pull loads of coal in the mines. I pass the bachelor band first – four mop-top colts skulking together near the bottom of the hill. I pass the two smallest and most recently formed harems: one belongs to Witness and consists of a mare and two foals; the other, with two mares and a foal, belongs to Garth. These two young ponies snagged their mares just last year, after a busy senior stallion failed to get them pregnant. After climbing past them, I reach two mature harems, Scott's (three mares, five foals, and an assistant) and then Hershey's (four mares and eight foals) in a cluster near the top of the hill. At the very top, the biggest harem of all – three mares and eleven foals under the ranking harem stallion, Herbie – has taken over the shed. Nobody seems remotely interested in challenging Herbie's right to this prime real estate, and his clan looks out from its shelter, dry, comfy, and unashamed, like hilltop Angeleños enjoying the knockout view.

Herbie arrived at New Bolton with an 'H' branded into his left hip; that's how he wound up with his name. He's a dapple-gray horse with a flaxen mane and a laid-back management style, and when I first meet him, as I'm tromping after Sue McDonnell through the herd, he's grazing unconcernedly by the fence while his mares and foals spread out in a loose and rambling group. 'Herbie's very relaxed, but he's one of the toughest suckers I've ever seen,' McDonnell says. His dominance has a positive carryover to his harem, and his young foals are confident and independent. 'He's just so cool. He can let them go down there' – McDonnell points to a couple of his yearlings playing around by Hershey's foals – 'and he can whip anybody's ass that goes near them.'

I first saw McDonnell all dressed up to speak to a University of Pennsylvania alumni group. In her big glasses and sensible slacks, she looked as if she'd just dropped in from a church bake sale, but she quickly dispelled any such notion when she began her lecture. 'Originally, I set out to study male sexual dysfunction – using the traditional rat model,' she said, waking up the retired vet in the bolo tie in front of me. At the recommendation of a professor, McDonnell switched to horses, and now she's the country's leading therapist for dysfunctional stallions. She spends a lot of the spring on call, jetting from one breeding shed to the next, helping stallions and stallion handlers whenever problems arise. (For those with a further interest, I recommend her paper 'Libido, Erection, and Ejaculatory Dysfunction in Stallions'.)

McDonnell has found that harem stallions in a 'free-running' herd are remarkably functional, in terms of both their psychological health and their reproductive effectiveness. They're sexually trouble-free, virile, and well behaved, with high libidos. Ninety per cent of the time they get their mares pregnant on the first heat after they give birth – the foal heat. (This is partly because if they don't, the mares will go find a stallion who can. As McDonnell says, 'A mare in heat is an attractive menace. It's just good harem management to nail them the first time.') In fact, while it's impossible to recreate harem conditions on a Thoroughbred breeding farm, McDonnell often takes the lessons that she's learned from harem stallions like Herbie and applies them to dysfunctional Kentucky stallions.

One of the simplest lessons involves testosterone. Perhaps not surprisingly, as soon as a stallion gains access to a harem, his testosterone level (and his reproductive readiness) goes way up. When he is deprived of that harem, his readings plummet to gelding level – he might as well be castrated. Give him the harem back, and his testosterone skyrockets. Take it away, and once again he's a mope. Apparently, access to mares works like an on-off switch for testosterone. One of the surprising corollaries of this finding is that, frequently, the horses with the highest testosterone levels at a breeding farm are the teaser stallions, who tend to live in and around broodmare barns, for on-the-spot teasing. McDonnell has found that many sexual dysfunctions simply disappear if the stallions are brought into continuous exposure to mares – in other words, if the studs are allowed to be more like the teasers – and the testosterone is left to do the rest.

Notice that it's the exposure to mares (not the frequency of copulation) that raises testosterone levels. Twice since the New

Bolton herd began, a stallion has voluntarily allied himself to a harem, taking up a position as a sort of assistant harem stallion – even though he was no more likely to get sex out of the deal than he would have been back in the bachelor band. But tests show that these assistants have the same high testosterone levels as the harem stallions, and undergo the same behavioral and physiological changes. They bulk up with muscle and grow more dominant and aggressive.

As an example of this testosterone kick, McDonnell points to Herbie, who's noticeably better built than his peers. But despite his obvious masculinity, he's not jumpy or violent, like some weight-lifter in a steroid rage. 'If you watch Herbie, you won't see him react a lot,' she says. 'He can direct other horses' behavior with very little – it's almost just a little toss of the head, or a little wave – you know, like the Godfather.'

McDonnell has changed from lecturing dress into boots and khakis to take me around the herd. She's a big, strong woman who grew up on a dairy farm in Lackawanna County, north of Scranton, and she bewails the lack of 'big country girls' like herself in veterinary programs – she gets too many students who are frail, vegetarian types. At one point, she praises a tough colleague by saying, 'She could hunt bear with a switch.' The compliment would work just as well for McDonnell.

She has a delightfully wicked laugh, and she's chosen a profession where she has plenty of opportunity to use it. She laughs about the old vet at the lecture who seemed so keenly interested in the homosexual behavior of the bachelor band. As the vet and I learned, stallions are eager bisexuals until they get their own harem, after which point they settle down to a life of contented heterosexuality. She laughs about being a laughingstock: for five years, before she began the herd, she studied 'this behavior called masturbation in horses'. She says it proved to be a great model to study the effect of certain erection-producing compounds (the forerunners of Viagra) with implications for human medicine. She says, 'People around here would be like, "Oh, I saw one of your horses. He had his thing out!" ' She laughs like a teenager.

'But it turned out to be a really wonderful tool for looking at an erection in a sexual context. I mean, you can actually get little pressure gauges and stuff. And they do this behavior every ninety minutes. And even on video, you can quantify and rate the number of bounces, the degree of tumescence, the degree of flare of the glans penis. And there are superimposed medications that you hope affect erection one way or the other. And you have this beautiful, peaceful visual model.'

As a scientist, McDonnell says, she doesn't attribute much cognitive ability to horses, because she doesn't have any evidence, for or against. 'And I don't need it to explain their behavior.' McDonnell's great at explaining their behavior: she's a practiced observer and a shrewd judge of equine character. When we come up to the bachelor band, she grows nostalgic. This year the band is only a quartet – she culled fifteen from the group last year, placing them on local farms at the end of a yearlong study of bachelors – and she clearly misses the trouble the larger band caused. 'There used to be a big group of them ready to challenge a harem stallion at every moment, so it's a lot quieter now. These four are clearly non-threatening.'

The bachelors' sexual ambition makes them look both hopeless and hyperaware. I ask her if it's like having teenagers around.

She hesitates: 'More like middle-aged single moms who are always waiting for an opportunity.'

Yet apparently opportunities do arise for the bachelors, and they don't even have to take over a harem to enjoy them. Under normal circumstances, young maidens live with their parents, moving with the harem under the protection of the stallion. But because there seems to be some natural prohibition against incest, McDonnell says, as soon as the maidens come into estrus the harem stallion stops policing them. 'And those females will go off and join the bachelors and get bred over and over. They'll go out, get bred. A half-hour later, you'll see them back with their families. Another half-hour later, they're back with the bachelors and they get bred again. Teenage behavior.'

McDonnell points out a young maiden mare from Hershey's harem, who's standing beside Testimony, the assistant harem stallion under Scott. 'Hershey's letting her be over there with Testimony,' she says, guessing that the mare has come into heat. Testimony, a black-and-white pony who normally stands guard over the harem and chases away the bachelors while Scott grazes with the mares, looks particularly alert just now. 'Testimony might get a little today. He hasn't in the past, but . . .'

Although winking at a daughter's promiscuity might not go down so well with the PTA, harem stallions do make surprisingly thoughtful and devoted fathers. Since mares in a herd spend more than eleven-twelfths of their adult life pregnant, nearly all their time has to be devoted to nursing, eating, and resting. So it's left to the harem stallion to handle most of the work of raising the young – settling disputes, setting examples, keeping an eye out for trouble, and simply playing with them. McDonnell says Herbie in particular seems to enjoy goofing around with his foals (although this pleasant leisure activity might be another benefit of his dominance: insecure stallions, like the rookies Garth and Witness, spend a lot of their time simply herding their harems out of Herbie's way).

'There's one cool thing I saw that really stimulated my thinking about how complex their relationships are,' McDonnell says, with her trademark mixture of excitement and scientific exactitude. 'On the whole, it seems like the babies born this year really like to get together and play. And so their families tend to position themselves around them while the babies sort of play in the middle. And I saw this episode – I actually stayed in the fields all day when I started to see it. They would have one stallion go in the middle as a sort of protector and he'd be the baby-sitter. Then, after a time, another stallion would come out and they would have this little exchange of guards. And one would go home and the other one would stay for a while.'

This is hardly what I'd expected: you get your own harem and suddenly the most noteworthy accomplishment in your life is child-care arrangements. 'When I saw this with those stallions, I could hardly believe it,' McDonnell says. 'They were actually cooperating. And you wonder what kind of communication there was on that. Did that all just happen? How did they schedule? There was just so much going on there that was very complex.'

The next day, I get up just before dawn and drive out to the herd because McDonnell says that's when the horses are most active. She also says that Kennett Square has the world's highest concentration of Lyme-disease-carrying ticks, so I've got two pairs of socks and a plastic bag on each foot, and I've tied the laces from my dress shoes around the cuffs of my pants. If this were a school field trip I'd be embarrassed, but at this hour it's just me and the horses and the break of day.

I carefully close the gate to the field and walk up a hill through the dewy knee-high grass. I can't see or hear a single horse. In fact, I'm looking down at my soaking-wet jeans, marveling at how dry my feet are inside the plastic bags when a bachelor rushes over the top of gully and nearly knocks me down. Another of his bachelor friends follows a split second later. But by the time I hurry to safe, low ground to look back at them, the bachelors have stopped running and instead stand together gazing wistfully across the large field at the harems spread out to graze. Posing at the top of the hill with their long pony bangs obscuring their eyes, they actually do look like a band: Herman's Hermits, say.

I open the folding canvas chair that McDonnell has lent me and sit down. I don't have to wait too long before I catch a stud-pile showdown between Witness, one of the rookie harem stallions, and Hershey, the number two stallion after Herbie. If the bachelors look like a British invasion band, Hershey looks like a mid-eighties metalhead, with luxurious rocker hair that flies up in the air when he runs – a scary sight if it weren't so pretty. When one of Witness's brood starts nosing over toward me to investigate, Hershey heads him off, and Witness comes over to stick up for his boy. The two stallions pose side by side, arching their necks like swans or warhorses. In short, they're just standing there, until Witness kicks – with his hind legs, in the empty air – and Hershey backs him down. Most of the confrontations that I see seem to follow this pattern: two horses freeze side by side in the semblance of fury, then one of them, generally the one who winds up losing, makes a face-saving aggressive gesture and backs away. In this case, Hershey sums up the neighborly disagreement with a fecal briquette. Witness waits patiently, then replies in kind. This poop-off is followed by a volley of snorts, which I swear ends when Hershey perfectly mimics the sound of Witness's snort, as if to mock his hollow tone and claims of triumph.

A little while later, I see two chestnut colts playing roughly with three black colts from another harem. I don't know who belongs to what group, but I can guess, because apparently horses can be just as superficial as people: they, too, tend to congregate according to skin color. Garth, for example, is butterscotch colored and so are his mares; Herbie is dapple-gray and his mares are dark; Scott keeps an inclusive harem with black-and-white horses, chestnuts, and bays; and as you might expect, Hershey favors the dark-chocolate types. At first, the two chestnuts and their three dark playmates seem to be having an uproarious time, rearing and shadowboxing with their front legs and crashing together softly in the air. But anybody who's taken a long drive with a big family knows how these things go: the laughter and roughhousing lift everybody's spirits for a while, and then there's a sick cracking sound and an instant of dead silence. I'm watching the whole thing (the alternative is to watch the chewing of grass) so, after the crack of contact, I see the black colt hit the ground and shake his head like a stunned boxer out on his feet, as the chestnut colt backs away. I doubt that any bones are broken, but the line between play and violence has been crossed.

Herbie races down from the top of the hill and herds his three black colts up to safety, leaving the two chestnut colts all by themselves. They stand in the middle of the field, enduring what looks to me like pointed isolation for a while, and then Witness, the lowest of all the stallions, comes out to chase them away, as if the task of threatening falls naturally to the most threatened. When he gives chase, they run off to the bachelor band. The two chestnut exiles pose there on the hill, gazing longingly back at the herd for a while just like the other bachelors. When they try to creep back to the herd, Hershey, their father, rushes up to repeat the verdict: he, too, chases them away.

For the rest of the morning, they play with the bachelors, and as I'm leaving for breakfast, I spot the horse who almost knocked me down when I arrived. He's trying to mount one of the chestnut newcomers.

Kennett Square lies in a rich crescent of colonial history. You see roadside markers everywhere, explaining, for instance, exactly how Cornwallis beat Washington in the Battle of Brandywine. You can visit the battleground: it's now a small state park and popular make-out spot. The locals seem comfortable living with the stuff. On the way to breakfast, I pass a woman in Puritan garb and sneakers chatting with a man in a Volvo. They kiss; then she stands by a butter churn while the man pulls out of the parking lot and drives away.

In the closest town, West Chester, near the corner of High and Gay Streets, I sit in a muffin shop. I'm all by myself, but I keep putting down my coffee and morning paper as if I've been interrupted. What about Blindman, the bachelor who nearly ran me down: how many of the horses know he's blind in one eye? Just yesterday morning, I saw him wandering through the herd, picking a fight with one stallion after the other until finally Herbie started chasing him up and down and back and forth. After three circuits through the high grass on their improvised oval, Herbie just stopped and Blindman scattered for good, back to the bachelors. You couldn't tell how seriously they took it, or, to the extent that they did, who had got the better of whom.

A little while later, I start to wonder about Witness. After he chased off the chestnut colts, he passed my folding chair on the way back to his harem. As soon as he saw me, he made the one gesture McDonnell had warned me about: head down, spine aimed at me like a knife, and coming on strong. I stood up and nodded politely, as if offering my seat, which seemed to satisfy him. He picked up his head and stepped on by, as if we'd come to an understanding. He didn't bother me again.

And yesterday, while I was watching the various harems and politely giving ground to do so, I somehow got maneuvered into the middle of the bachelor band. What was that all about? Is that where they think I belong?

I put down my coffee again and laugh out loud. I've been sitting here neglecting the sports pages for the past hour, thinking about horses in the gossipy way I think about the people at work, replaying encounters over coffee and passing judgment. It's easy to get caught up in it all. And just like work, the herd is a small place where it's impossible, even unwise, not to have opinions.

The next morning, a rainstorm hits. It comes down so hard that the horses stop moving, except for all their invisible shuffle steps when the wind shifts. They keep their heads down mostly, so the rain can find a groove through their coats and roll off. Up in the run-in shed, Herbie and his harem aren't moving either. They stand with the unnatural stillness of people crammed together in the subway, wary and unreadable.

But you can feel the mood lift when the rain lets up to a light drizzle. First, the youngest horses start to play with each other, friendly nibbles and pinches that bring out frolicsome answering kicks. Then a pair of young showoffs start chasing each other through the herd, jumping and bucking, with the pony in pursuit staying so close to his friend's tail that whenever the lead horse bucks, the kicks slip harmlessly by on either side of his friend's neck. They seem to like this trick: they try it a lot. Then they trade places and try it some more.

McDonnell says that every time there's a big change in weather – the first snow, a sudden thaw, the break in a heat wave, or like today, the first rain of the year – the horses get giddy and excited. For the newest foals, it's the first rain of their lives, and the skinny one- or two-month-olds take off and skitter over the wet grass and try sliding to a stop in the mud. The older generations set out after them, the first time I've seen the herd following the lead of its youngest members. Older juveniles try mounting one another, and this show of youthful concupiscence seems to inspire Herbie, who walks slowly over to his foundation mare, Splash, and gives her a nudge. She's having none of it, and Herbie seems to know better than to ask twice.

As the rains stops, the herd scatters into the various harems. I watch Garth, in just his second breeding season, grazing beside Peanut, his foundation mare. He, too, sees something encouraging and heads straight to her side, getting close enough to put his lips and nose along her neck. In reply, Peanut rears up and gives him a good hard kick in the chest. Garth stands there considering; then he shrugs and goes back to grazing beside her. The couple stands very close. You can tell they've been over this before.

Despite their impressive résumés in the field, I haven't seen any of the harem stallions actually engaging in any sex. Maybe none of the mares came into heat during my visit. Maybe they don't want me to see it. McDonnell has told me how easy it is to miss the sex act. The herd's usually spread out and the hills are full of hiding places and anyway it's over fast. But the main reason I won't catch them having sex, she says, is because 'it's so quiet and unobtrusive. Because when the stallions are there all the time, there's no need for that great, flamboyant entrance'.

Quiet, frequent, amid rebuffs and the misbehavior of children: I hadn't expected the sex life of a harem stallion to sound so much like the married version. Fine. We've seen enough by now, and I can appreciate their discretion. If they like it quiet, I'll shut up.

ACKNOWLEDGEMENTS

My thanks to David Remnick and Karen Rinaldi, who gave me the chance to write about studs, first as an article in *The New Yorker* and now as a Bloomsbury book; Alice Truax and Lara Carrigan, who gave it shape, and Tina Bennett, who made it possible; my friends and coworkers, for listening to stories about horse sex over lunch; the staff of Overbrook Farm, who saw too much of me; and my best friends, who haven't seen me at all lately. Finally and especially, thanks to my wife, Amy, who showed me from the very beginning that this was a love story.

ABOUT THE AUTHOR

Kevin Conley is an editor at *The New Yorker*. His writing has appeared in the *New York Times Sunday Magazine*, *Sports Illustrated*, and *The New Yorker*. He lives in Brooklyn with his wife, Amy, and their two children, Max and Sarah.

A NOTE ON THE TYPE

The text of this book is set in Bembo. This type was first used in 1495 by the Venetian printer Aldus Manutius for Cardinal Bembo's *De Aetna*, and was cut for Manutius by Francesco Griffo. It was one of the types used by Claude Garamond (1480– 1561) as a model for his Romain de l'Université, and so it was the forerunner of what became standard European type for the following two centuries. Its modern form follows the original types and was designed for Monotype in 1929.